The Changing Military Balance in the Gulf

Andrew Rathmell

Royal United Services Institute for Defence Studies

First Published 1996

© Royal United Services Institute for Defence Studies

All rights reserved. No part of this publication may be reproduced, stored in a retrieval system, or transmitted in any form or by any means, electronic, mechanical, photocopying, recording or otherwise, without prior permission of the Royal United Services Institute for Defence Studies.

ISBN 0-85516-145-0
ISSN 0268-1307

The Royal United Services Institute for Defence Studies (RUSI) is a professional body based in London dedicated to the study, analysis and debate of issues affecting defence and international security.

Founded in 1831 by the Duke of Wellington, the RUSI is one of the most senior institutes of its kind in the world which, throughout its history, has been at the forefront of contemporary political-military thinking through debates, public and private seminars, conferences, lectures and a wide range of publications. The independence of the Institute is guaranteed by a large, worldwide membership of those people and organisations who have a serious and professional interest in the thorough and objective analysis of defence and international security.

Critical and acclaimed analysis of issues of the moment has underwritten the RUSI's Whitehall Papers for many years. The new series will, in its revised A5 monograph format, continue to provide expertise in the field. The series, which will comprise six publications a year, will address the major areas of current interest.

Whitehall Papers are available as part of a membership package, or singly at £6.50 plus p & p (£1.00 in the UK/ £2.00 overseas). Orders should be sent to the Publications Department, RUSI, Whitehall, London SW1A 2ET and cheques and postal orders made payable to the RUSI.

Printed in Great Britain by Sherrens Printers, Units 1 & 2, South Park, Granby Industrial Estate, Weymouth, Dorset.
The Royal United Services Institute for Defence Studies, Whitehall, London SW1A 2ET.
Registered Charity No. 210639

CONTENTS

Introduction		1
Chapter 1	Iran	9
Chapter 2	Iraq	24
Chapter 3	Saudi Arabia	36
Chapter 4	The Other GCC States	50
Chapter 5	Measuring the Balance	80
Geostrategic Weights		81
Relative Militarisation		82
Military Capabilities		85
Bean-counting		86
Net Assessment		95
Chapter 6	Conclusions	105
Charts		111
Appendices		121

I.   Geo-strategic Weights
II. Relative Militarisation
III Military Capability
IV ADE Calculations
V.   Effect of Close Air Support

ACKNOWLEDGEMENTS

The initial research for this paper was assisted by grants from the University of Exeter and the British Academy. The study benefited from comments and at seminars hosted by the School of Oriental and African Studies, Wilton Park, the 1996 EURAMES Conference and RUSI.

Dr Andrew Rathmell is Deputy Director of the International Centre for Security Analysis (ICSA), Department of War Studies, King's College London. He is author of *Secret War in the Middle East: The Covert Struggle for Syria, 1949-1961* (London: I.B. Tauris, 1995) and editor *of Gulf States Newsletter.*

ABBREVIATIONS

ACDA	Arms Control and Disarmament Agency
ADE	Armoured Division Equivalent
ATGW	Anti-Tank Guided Weapon
AIFV	Armoured Infantry Fighting Vehicle
APC	Armoured Personnel Carrier
ARV	Armoured Reconnaissance Vehicle
C^3I	Command, Control, Communications and Intelligence
FGA	Fighter Ground Attack
GDP	Gross Domestic Product
IISS	International Institute for Strategic Studies
IRGC	Iranian Revolutionary Guard Corps
JCSS	Jaffee Center for Strategic Studies
LST	Landing Ship (Tank)
MBT	Main Battle Tank
MCM	Mine Counter Measures
MRL	Multiple Rocket Launcher
RCL	Recoilless Rifle
RL	Rocket Launcher
SAM	Surface to Air Missile
SANG	Saudi Arabian National Guard
SIPRI	Stockholm International Peace Research Institute
SSM	Surface-to-Surface Missile
SSR	Surface-to-Surface Rocket
WEI	Weapon Effectiveness Index
WUV	Weighted Unit V

INTRODUCTION

In 1996 the Gulf is no nearer to having a stable regional security system than it was three years ago when RUSI last published a Whitehall Paper on Gulf Security. That paper concluded that 'Gulf security is a hostage to the nature of the governments involved. The result is a stand-off ... Collective security is nowhere in sight. Instead, Western intervention is holding the line, by isolating Iraq, containing Iran and bolstering the GCC.'[1]

This conclusion reflects the conventional wisdom in Western capitals as well as in the Gulf Cooperation Council (GCC) states themselves. This is that, in the absence of fundamental political change in Iraq and Iran, stability and the security of the GCC states can only be ensured by a strong Western military presence to deter Iraq and Iran.[2] In line with this policy, Western forces, led by the US, are digging in for a long haul in the Gulf. Since the 'Bottom Up' review of US defence planning, the Pentagon sees a conventional military threat from Iran or Iraq as one of its two canonical conflict scenarios.[3] In response to this threat it has been prepositioning equipment in the region and has accelerated the tempo of air, land and sea exercises.[4] Britain and France have done likewise, though inevitably on a more limited scale.[5]

At the same time the GCC states are in the midst of massive rearmament programmes and are reshaping their armed forces in the name of self-sufficiency. The region is no longer the booming conventional arms market it once was, with estimated deliveries of major weapons systems having fallen from a peak of over $15 billion in 1987 to just over $5 billion in 1994.[6] Nonetheless, the evident failings of the GCC armed forces in the Gulf War,[7] together with the need to lock in their Western protectors by purchasing equipment, led to the six GCC states accounting for over 11 per cent of the value of global arms transfers between 1990 and 1994.[8]

There would appear to be a contradiction between these two developments. If the Western powers judge that only the forward presence of their troops can deter Iran and Iraq, then why should the GCC states put so much effort into their military programmes? This question is increasingly being asked in the Gulf itself. Some Kuwaiti parliamentarians have been especially vociferous in their protests at what they see as wasteful expenditure.[9] Saudi Islamist dissidents have meanwhile attacked their government's reliance on Western forces, chastising the government for not building strong enough national forces.[10]

One explanation for the contradiction is that GCC states purchase arms for reasons unrelated to defence. This is true to some extent.[11] Nonetheless, the GCC states' military establishments are genuinely seeking to improve their combat potential and thereby their deterrent capabilities. It is not, on the face of it, obvious why they should be unable to field military forces sufficient to deter a future Iraqi or Iranian threat.

Too often observers in the West and the Gulf appear to assume that, no matter what they do, the GCC states will never be able to defend themselves.[12] This pessimistic view appears to be based on three assumptions. First, that Iraq and Iran's populations, 21 million and 64.8 million, so outweigh the GCC's, 24.9 million, that the latter can never hope to match either of its neighbours in terms of mobilised manpower.[13] Second, that a lack of bellicosity among the pampered populations of the GCC states makes them less effective warriors than the Iraqis or Iranians. Third, that the limited technological and organisational skills of the GCC militaries make them unable to effectively use their costly imported equipment.

While these caveats have some force, such generalisations are an insufficient basis on which to judge the prospects for a stable balance of military power in the Gulf. In order to arrive at a more accurate

Introduction

forecast of the future regional balance, it is desirable to apply more rigorous and systematic analytical techniques.

The aim of this paper, then, is to study the changing capabilities of the Gulf's military forces and to assess what impact force building plans may have on the regional military balance.

Gulf security: no new thinking

The international security agenda has been changing rapidly across the globe in recent years. Gorbachev's 'new thinking' on security coincided with a reconsideration of the international security agenda in Western circles. A reduced emphasis on military forces and a broader definition of security to include economic and environmental factors have been key elements in this new thinking.[14] The decline of a traditional realist perception of international relations and an end to 'zero-sum' notions of national security and inter-state competition has allowed more room for notions of collective security. This rethinking process, together with an acceptance of the existing systemic correlation of forces, helped bring about the Arab-Israeli peace process.[15]

This conceptual reorientation has however not yet permeated into official thinking in and on the Gulf.[16] The three poles of power—Iraq, Iran and Saudi Arabia—continue to see their relations as a 'zero-sum' competition.[17] Worse, both Iraq and Iran are revisionist powers who do not accept the existing correlation of forces. The persistence of these approaches to security means that the best way to analyse Gulf security is through a balance of power approach, however antiquated this notion may seem to advocates of the new international security agenda.

In terms of balance of power, Gulf security and stability have in the recent past been ensured by the presence of a hegemonic power.[18] Britain performed this role until its withdrawal in 1971. During the 1970s Imperial Iran, backed by the US, took over. It dominated Iraq, forcing it to sign the Algiers Accord in 1975, and helped Oman crush the Dhofar insurgency. Since the Gulf War, the US has taken on the mantle of regional hegemon.

When the regional strategic balance has been upset, opportunities have then arisen for aggression. Iraq's invasions of Iran (1980) and Kuwait (1990) were in part motivated by the Iraqi leadership's perception of the existence of a favourable balance of military power– a window of strategic opportunity.

Although there is much talk of a regional security structure for the Gulf, a basic assumption of this paper is that work can only begin on such a project once a strategic balance is established between the three regional poles.[19] In a regional system where none of the leading states will accept to be subordinate to its neighbours, collective security and confidence building measures can only really be effective once a balance of power is established. Moreover, it needs to be seen to be established.

Analysing the balance

The conventional military balance is only one component of the military balance of power, and the balance of power is only one component of strategic stability. Nonetheless, as a starting point, this study will focus on the conventional military balance.

It is recognised that foreign, notably US, military forces will dominate the balance of power in the Gulf in the coming years. The level of these forces is a vital component of the regional balance as is the ease of sustaining and reinforcing them. However, this factor is not a central concern of this study. It is clear that US diplomatic and military muscle will ensure 'stability' (i.e. the *status quo*) in the near future.[20] The purpose of this study is, on the other hand, to analyse the intra-regional military balances that are evolving beneath this umbrella. The currently overwhelming US military presence is

Introduction

unlikely to last indefinitely and, in the meantime, the changing regional balance could have a dramatic impact on regional relations.

This main focus of this paper is on ground forces and close air support. The regional air and naval balance is discussed only briefly. This is because the modelling tools applied here are unsuitable for analysing the latter balances and an extension of the study to incorporate further models would either have made it too long or would have necessitated cutting drastically discussion of several very interesting developments in the ground force balance. Likewise, non-conventional weapons developments are not discussed. Omitting this aspect allows for a clearer focus on key conventional weapons developments.

The paper has two components. The first four chapters describe the force building and acquisition plans of Iran, Iraq, Saudi Arabia and the smaller GCC states. Chapter five assesses trends in the current and future military balance by using two quantitative techniques–bean counting and net assessment with the Weapon Effectiveness Indices/Weighted Unit Value (WEI/WUV) methodology.[21]

Sources

An initial problem in this research was compiling the basic data relating to equipment inventories. There are generally accepted databases which derive from a mixture of official sources, press accounts and statements from governments and opposition groups in the region.[22] Virtually all sources are, however, inconsistent in themselves and with each other.[23] In this research, an attempt was made to synthesise data from a variety of open published sources, supplemented by interviews with a number of Western officials. Nonetheless, especially for Iran and Iraq, the figures should be taken as estimates rather than as accurate accountings of arsenals.

In all tables of equipment inventories, the totals of current holdings have been derived from a combination of *The Military Balance*, *The Middle East Military Balance* and Jane's *Sentinel*. Predictions of equipment holdings have been compiled from a combination of press articles, government documentation and interviews.

Notes

1. R. Hollis, *Gulf Security: No Consensus*, Whitehall Paper 20 (London, Royal United Services Institute, 1993), p. 71.
2. H.F. Eilts, 'The US Perception of Arabian Gulf Security,' *Asian Affairs*, October 1994, pp. 270-280.
3. W. J. Clinton, *National Security Strategy of the United States, 1994-1995* (Washington, DC, Brassey's, 1995), pp. 27-28; S. Simon, 'US Strategy in the Persian Gulf,' *Survival*, Vol. 34, No. 3 (Autumn 1992), pp. 81-97.
4. 'In Heart of Gulf, US Fleet Keeps Wary Eye on Saddam,' *International Herald Tribune* (hereafter *IHT*), 31 January 1996; 'US Military Presence in Persian Gulf,' *Defense News*, 19-25 December 1994.
5. "Iron Magic' works to sharpen region's skills,' *Jane's Military Exercise & Training Monitor*, January-March 1996, pp. 8-10.
6. For the purposes of this study, conventional arms include 'weapons-related technologies' and 'conventional dual-use technologies.' For a discussion of definitions, see: P. Eavis and O. Sprague, 'Conventional Weapons Proliferation and Control,' in Deltac Ltd/Saferworld, *Proliferation and Export Controls* (London, Doveton Press, 1995), p. 80. Figures for 1980s are Cordesman's derivation's of ACDA figures. A.H. Cordesman, *After the Storm: The Changing Military Balance in the Middle East* (Westview Press, Boulder, CO, 1993), p. 38. Figures for 1990-1994 arms transfers are from SIPRI Yearbooks 1994 and 1995. Stockholm International Peace Research Institute, *Armaments, Disarmament and International Security* (Oxford, Oxford University Press). For an interpretation of arms sales trends, see: A. Karp, 'The Demise of the Middle East Arms Race,' *The Washington Quarterly*, Vol. 18, No. 4 (1995), pp. 29-51.
7. The term Gulf War is used to refer to the 1990-91 war over Kuwait in distinction to the 1980-88 Iran-Iraq War.
8. East and South East Asia, the other booming arms market, accounted for 20 per cent of global arms transfers in this period. SIPRI Yearbook 1995, *Armaments, Disarmament and International Security*, pp. 492-496.
9. 'Kuwait to resume arms buying under MPs' scrutiny,' *Reuter*, 27 March 1994.
10. R.H. Dekmejian, 'The Rise of Political Islamism in Saudi Arabia,' *Middle East Journal*, Vol. 48, No. 4 (Autumn 1994), pp. 627-643.
11. Four major motivations for arms acquisition, aside from purely military needs, can be identified: a) domestic politics; for instance the need to keep

military establishments satisfied; b) diplomatic; for instance the desire by GCC states to consolidate their diplomatic alliances with arms purchases; c) prestige and posturing; for instance it has been suggested that Qatar purchased the Mirage 2000-5 mainly in order to outdo its rival Bahrain which had purchased F-16s; d) personal interest; including commissions and personal ties between senior officials and arms supplying companies and countries.

12. See for instance, R.G. Mainuddin, J.R. Aicher, Jr. and J.M. Elliot, 'From Alliance to Collective Security: Rethinking the Gulf Cooperation Council,' *Middle East Policy*, Vol. 4, No. 3 (March 1996), pp. 39-49; M. Ziarati, 'The defence of Arabia after the Gulf war,' *Middle East International* (hereafter *MEI*), 7 February 1992, pp. 19-20.

13. Population figures are taken from IISS, *The Military Balance* 1995 (London, IISS, 1995) for the sake of consistency. It should be noted that there are serious doubts about the accuracy of these figures.

14. On this debate, see: B. Buzan, *People, States and Fear: An Agenda for International Security in the Post-Cold War Era* (New York, Harvester Wheatsheaf, 1991); J. Chipman, 'The Future of Strategic Studies,' *Survival*, Vol. 34, No. 1 (1992), pp. 109-131.

15. A less benign interpretation is provided by A. Hashim, 'The State, Society, and the Evolution of Warfare in the Middle East: The Rise of Strategic Deterrence?' *The Washington Quarterly*, Vol. 18, No. 4 (1995), pp. 53-72.

16. S.T. Hunter, 'Persian Gulf Security: Lessons of the Past and the Need for New Thinking,' *SAIS Review*, Vol. 12, No. 1 (Winter/Spring 1992), pp. 155-166; A. Munro, 'Gulf Security–the War and its Aftermath,' *RUSI Journal*, August 1993, pp. 6-17.

17. For the sake of simplicity, this study only considers the balance of power among states bordering the Gulf. It is, however, clear that the dynamics of the wider Middle East mean that Israel, Turkey, Pakistan and India have an impact on the strategic balance.

18. J.E. Peterson, *Defending Arabia* (London, Croom Helm, 1986).

19. As pointed out in a 1989 study by Chatham House. P. Robins, *The Future of the Gulf: Politics and Oil in the 1990s* (London, Royal Institute of International Affairs, 1989), p. 75.

20. At least against external threats. Whether the US presence will exacerbate the GCC states' internal problems is another matter. G. Bahgat, 'Military Security and Political Stability in the Gulf,' *Arab Studies Quarterly*, Vol. 17, No. 4 (Fall 1995), pp. 55-70. Terrorist bombings in November 1995 and June 1996 in Saudi Arabia suggest that this may become

an increasing problem. 'Few See Saudi Stability Threatened by Militants', *Washington Post*, 27 June 1996.

21. For discussions of the problems associated with assessing military balances, see: J.J. Mearsheimer, 'Numbers, Strategy, and the European Balance,' *International Security*, Vol. 12, No. 4 (Spring 1988), pp. 174-185 and K.R. Holmes, 'Measuring the Conventional Balance in Europe,' *International Security*, Vol. 12, No. 4 (Spring 1988), pp. 166-173.

22. The main ones being: International Institute for Strategic Studies (IISS), Stockholm International Peace Research Institute (SIPRI), Arms Control and Disarmament Agency (ACDA), Jaffee Center for Strategic Studies (JCSS) and Jane's Information Group. In the Gulf, the UN Register on Conventional Arms is of limited use as regional powers have been reluctant to make returns. M. Chalmers and O. Greene, 'The UN Register of Conventional Arms: The Third Year of Operation,' paper presented to BISA Annual Conference, December 1995.

23. For instance, considering 1995 figures for Iran's stock of combat aircraft one finds that the IISS lists a total of 295, while Jane's *Sentinel* lists 388. For Iraq, IISS lists 316 while Jane's lists 171.

CHAPTER 1
IRAN

The Islamic Republic of Iran finds itself in a threatening security environment but the isolation of Iraq has left it with a security window of several years with no immediate Iraqi threat. Iraq nonetheless remains the main external threat to the Iranian regime. Even if Saddam Hussein were removed, it is hard to see the two countries not arming themselves against each other. Iran suffered badly in human terms from its lack of military equipment during the Iran-Iraq War and knows that Iraq retains significant conventional military potential. Although it has a grace period, Iran needs to be able to deter or defeat a revitalised Iraqi military. Iran also feels threatened by the military build up in the Gulf, especially that of US forces.[1] This is partly because Iran believes it has a natural right to dominate the Gulf. In addition, though, Tehran recalls the ease with which the US Navy hit its oil installations and naval forces in 1987-8. For Iran, the American threat to its oil export lifeline is a real one. Israel is also a potential threat. Elsewhere, Iran is nervous of instability in Afghanistan and of a spillover of the fighting in the Caucasus. At the same time, Tehran cannot ignore the nuisance value of the *Mujahidin-i Khalq* and the potential spillover from Kurdish fighting in northern Iraq.[2]

In response to these multiple threats, Iran has sought to modernise and professionalise its armed forces.[3] Emphasis has been placed on building a modern military, capable of conducting combined arms offensive and defensive operations. This training and restructuring programme has been accompanied by a large-scale procurement effort. This re-equipment was necessary since much of Iran's hardware was lost during the war against Iraq. In the final battles of summer 1988, Iran may have lost some 40 per cent of its major army equipment.

The Changing Military Balance in the Gulf

In order to make up its losses, Iran ordered some $6.7bn worth of new arms between 1989 and 1992. Deliveries totalled up to $4.5bn in this period, according to the CIA. Other sources such as the Congressional Research Service and SIPRI put Iran's deliveries rather differently as the following table shows. Russia has been the main supplier. Iran's largest orders were the June 1989 ($4bn) and July 1992 ($2.5bn) deals with Moscow. There has however been no evidence of deliveries under the 1992 deal as yet. Chinese deliveries, meanwhile, totalled $1.1bn in the same period.[4]

Estimated arms deliveries, ($ million) [5]

	1990	1991	1992	1993	1994
CIA	2000	2,000	?	?	?
CRS	1400	1500	300	?	?
SIPRI	776	175	283	1193	780

In addition to imports, Iran has made major efforts to develop an indigenous arms industry. Although not as successful as Tehran often claims, it has attained near self sufficiency in items such as ammunition and spares.[6] It has also been good at cannibalising equipment to keep its US aircraft operating and limited manufacturing capabilities have been demonstrated. Iran has displayed a domestic version of the Bell Jetranger configured as a helicopter gunship *(Zafar)* and the *Zulfiqar* MBT (probably based on the M-60).[7]

Ground Forces

During the Iran-Iraq War the revolutionary government downgraded the professional army in favour of the Iranian Revolutionary Guard Corps (IRGC) and scorned professional knowledge in favour of dedication and revolutionary élan.[8] This approach led to a high number of casualties, especially after Iran's armoured units were badly mauled–forcing a reliance on massed infantry assaults. Since the war, attempts have been made to counter these problems. The IRGC and the army have been more closely integrated with the formation of a joint Chiefs of Staff in 1992 and officers have been transferred between the two. The IRGC have been given formal rank structures and their professional training has improved. Their role, however, aside from control of Surface to Surface Missiles (SSM) and naval forces, is mainly as light infantry and internal security forces.

The army itself has become more proficient at combined arms operations and large scale manoeuvres. In the last couple of years it has carried out a series of exercises focusing on armoured warfare and on operating in a nuclear, biological and chemical environment.[9] Iran gives these exercises a lot of publicity in order to emphasise its military readiness. However, it is not clear whether Iran faces problems similar to Iraq in regard to the coordination of large scale operations. It is likely that its logistical and organisational back up are of a mediocre standard. It is also unclear just how effective this intensive cycle of exercises has been in preparing troops and staffs for combat.

In terms of equipment, Iran's armoured units still rely heavily on American M-60 and British Chieftain MBTs purchased by the Shah almost two decades ago. Their age and lack of spares has meant a low level of serviceability.[10] This force of Western MBTs has been supplemented by T-54/5s from the former East Germany and USSR, T-62s from North Korea, T-59s from China and T-72s from Russia.

Cordesman argues that Iran has decided to standardise on the T-72 and wants to deploy a force of 1500-2000 tanks by the year 2000.[11] Jane's *Sentinel*, however, suggests that Iran drew the lesson from the 1990-91 Gulf War that attack helicopters were making the tank obsolete and that tanks are being bought from Russia to maintain current fleet levels, but that 'the tank fleet would not be greatly expanded.'[12] The precise details of recent and planned tank purchases are shrouded in mystery. A comprehensive trade deal signed with the USSR in June 1989 may have included the supply of T-72s and it has been reported that 400-500 T-72s were ordered from Russia in March 1992. A further 200 T-72s may have been ordered from the Ukraine in 1992.[13] In 1995 Poland announced that it was going ahead with the sale of 100 T-72s, worth $30-40 million.[14] In 1990 it was reported that China had agreed to sell Iran Type 80 and Type 85 MBTs but no figures were given.[15] An agreement was also concluded with Czechoslovakia in 1989 for the purchase of 1500 T-55s but this may have lapsed as Iran decided not to acquire these obsolete weapons. In 1994, the Czech government announced that it had refused export licences for arms to Iran.[16]

MBT

Type	Role	1995	2000	2005
Zulfiqar	MBT	20?	20?	20?
T-72	MBT	200-250	1000	1000
T-54/5	MBT	110-250	110-250	110-250
T-62	MBT	50-150	50-150	50-150
Type 59	MBT	220-250	220-250	220-250
Type 69	MBT	70-200	70-200	70-200
Chieftain Mk3/5	MBT	40-250	40-250	40-250
M-47/8	MBT	90-150	90-150	90-150
M-60A1	MBT	50-160	50-160	50-160
Total	**MBT**	**1070-1440**	**1870-2370**	**1870-2370**

In addition to buying new tanks, Iran is upgrading the quality of its existing armour. India has agreed to upgrade Iran's tank guns and Hungary to refurbish T-55 engines. Yugoslavia has reportedly been installing T-72 engines in T-55s and equipping them with laser rangefinders.[17] In addition, Iran claims that it has upgraded captured Iraqi T-54s.[18]

For the purposes of this study, it is assumed that Iran deploys a force of 1000 T-72s by the year 2000, an additional 750-800. The efforts being made to upgrade Iran's older Soviet-style MBTs and to keep the Imperial-era MBTs operational indicate that Iran hopes to keep these in the arsenal in the medium term. Therefore, no phase outs of older tanks are assumed in the coming decade.

Iran hopes to supplement its tank forces with modern mechanised infantry units and is equipping itself with Russian BMP-2 AIFVs. Under the 1992 contract with Russia, Iran is reportedly acquiring 500 BMP-2s. In addition, China has assisted the IRGC with a $14 million spare parts programme for its BMP-1s.[19] Iran has produced the *Boraq* 4x4 APC domestically but it is unclear if this is operational.[20] This study assumes that Iran deploys 500 BMP-2s by the turn of the century but makes no further significant acquisitions.

ARV/AIFV/APC

Type	Role	1995	2000	2005
PT-76	ARV	90?	90?	90?
Scorpion	ARV	30-80	30-80	30-80
EE-9 Cascavel	ARV	39-85	39-85	39-85
BRDM-2	ARV	30?	30?	30?
Total	**ARV**	**119-235**	**119-235**	**119-235**
BMP-1	AIFV	90-300	90-300	90-300
BMP-2	AIFV	100?	500	500
Total	**AIFV**	**90-400**	**590-800**	**590-800**
BTR-152	APC	45?	45?	45?
BTR-40/50/60	APC	330?	330?	330?
M-113	APC	70?	70?	70?
Half-track	APC	90?	90?	90?
Total	**APC**	**535-550**	**535-550**	**535-550**

Despite the reported indigenous production of a self-propelled gun, Iran's artillery remains largely towed.[21] There are no reports of efforts to acquire towed or SP artillery pieces from abroad but the Iranians have been trying to deploy more sophisticated fire control systems.[22] Iran's domestic arms industry produces surface to surface rockets and MRLs.[23] This study assumes a modest addition to the

The Changing Military Balance in the Gulf

numbers of tube and MRL artillery pieces over the coming decade as a result of domestic production.

Surface to Surface Missiles

SS-1 Scud B/C	SSM	10 (210-350msl)	10 (210-350msl)	10 (210-350msl)
CSS-8	SSM	25 (200msl)?	25 (200msl)?	25 (200msl)?
Total	**SSM**	**35?**	**35?**	**35?**

Artillery

Type	Role	1995	2000	2005
FROG-7	SSR	250?	250?	250?
355mm *Nazeat*	SSR	500?	500?	500?
333mm *Shahin 2*	SSR	250?	250?	250?
320mm *Oghab*	SSR	200?	200?	200?
Total	**SSR**	**1200?**	**1200?**	**1200?**
203mm M110	SP How	18-30	18-30	18-30
175mm M1978	SP Gun	9-30	9-30	9-30
175mm M107	SP Gun	22-30	22-30	22-30
155mm M109/A1	SP How	85-160	85-160	85-160
122mm 2S1	SP How	18-60	18-60?	18-60?
Total	**SP Artillery**	**173-289**	**173-289**	**173-289**
203mm M115	Howitzer	20-25	20-25	20-25
155mm GH N-45	Gun (towed)	80-90	80-90	80-90
155mm WAC-21	Gun (towed)	15?	15?	15?
155mm M114	How (towed)	70-100	70-100	70-100
152mm D20	Gun (towed)	30?	30?	30?
130mm Type 59	Field Gun (towed)	50-1000	50-1000	50-1000

130mm M46	Field Gun (towed)	100?	100?	100?
122mm D-30	How (towed)	100-550	100-550	100-550
122mm Type 54	How (towed)	25-100	25-100	25-100
122mm Type 60	Gun (towed)	25?	25?	25?
105mm M56	How (towed)	20?	20?	20?
105mm M101A1	How (towed)	130-180	130-180	130-180
85mm D44	Field Gun (towed)	80?	80?	80?
75mm M116	How (towed)	115?	115?	115?
Total	**Towed Artillery**	**910-1995**	**910-2200**	**910-2200**
240mm M1985	MRL	9?	9?	9?
122mm BM11	MRL	5?	5?	5?
122mm BM21	MRL	45-100	45-100	45-100
122mm *Hadid*	MRL	50?	50?	50?
122mm Type 81	MRL	50?	50?	50?
107mm Type 63	MRL	90-500	90-500	90-500
Total	**MRL**	**185-664**	**200-700**	**200-700**
120mm DIO	Mortar	500?	500?	500?
120mm Soltam	Mortar	200?	200?	200?
107mm M30	Mortar	150?	150?	150?
81mm DIO	Mortar	900?	900?	900?
60mm	Mortar	500?	500?	500?
Total	**Mortar**	**2250-3500**	**2250-3500**	**2250-3500**

The Changing Military Balance in the Gulf

Anti-Tank Weapons

Type	Role	1995	2000	2005
106mm M40A1	RCL	200?	200?	200?
75mm M20	RCL	200?	200?	200?
57mm	RCL	150?	150?	150?
3.5in M20	RCL	50?	50?	50?
Total	RCL	**600?**	**600?**	**600?**
RPG-7V	RL	490?	490?	490?
Total	RL	**490?**	**490?**	**490?**
Shahine 1	ATGW	1000?	1000?	1000?
AT-3/4 *Sagger/Spigot*	ATGW	100?	100?	100?
Red Arrow 8	ATGW	100?	100?	100?
Dragon	ATGW	30?	30?	30?
BGM-71A	ATGW	250?	250?	250?
Entac	ATGW	90?	90?	90?
Total	ATGW	**1570?**	**1570?**	**1570?**

Army Aviation (Armed only)

Type	Role	1995	2000	2005
Bell AH-1J	Attack Helo	70-120	70-120	70-120
Mi-24	Attack Helo	10?	10?	10?
Zafar 300, Bell 206A	Attack Helo	?	?	?
Total	Attack Helo	80-130	80-130	80-130

Air Force

The Islamic Republic, like Imperial Iran, regards the air force as the main asset of its armed forces. The Iranian Air Force (IAF) performed well in the early months of the Iran-Iraq War before lack of parts grounded many of its US planes. During the war, Iran had to turn to whatever suppliers were around and bought F-6s and F-7s from China. These were obsolete when bought and have now mostly been given to the IRGC as light support aircraft. Iran would like to keep its large stock of US aircraft flying and is putting a lot of effort into keeping them in the air. However, lack of spares means that many are out of action. Iran has, as a result, turned to Russia. The Russian deliveries, along with the incorporation of some of the Iraqi jets that fled in 1991, have led to a major improvement of the Iranian Air Force with MiG-29 fighters and Su-24 long range strike aircraft.

Western analysts suggest that former air force chief Major General Mansour Sattari launched a 15 year modernisation plan in 1988 which envisaged building a force of 400 combat aircraft, built around the MiG-29 Fulcrum, the Su-24 Fencer and the MiG-31 Foxhound.[24]

The first two squadrons of MiG-29s were displayed in September 1990.[25] The July 1992 deal may have included orders for 12 Tu-22M Blinder bombers, 24 MiG-31 interceptors, 2 Mainstay Airborne Early Warning Aircraft, 48 MiG-29 fighters and 24 MiG-27 FGAs. The deal may also have included the An-72 maritime reconnaissance aircraft and the AS-6 antiship missile to be carried by Blinders. In addition, Russia reportedly agreed to refurbish the Iraqi Sukhois and MiGs that flew to Iran in 1991.[26]

Although all of the available estimates are unreliable, the cumulative total order from Russia may be for 50 MiG-29s and 36 Su-24s.[27] There has been no evidence as yet of the delivery of Tu-22s, MiG-31s or MiG-27s. Assuming no more of the Iraqi aircraft are incorporated into the inventory, then Iran is likely to field another 30 Fencers and another 24 MiG-29s by the year 2000. In light of Iran's current and projected financial difficulties, this study assumes that no more purchases are made before the end of the decade. It assumes, though, that the 1992 order is fulfilled by the year 2005.

Combat Aircraft[28]

Type	Role	1995	2000	2005
F-14 Tomcat	Fighter	15-60	15-60	15-60
F-6 (Ch MiG-19)	Fighter	20?	20?	20?
F-7 (Ch MiG-21)	Fighter	25-65	25-65	25-65
MiG-29 Fulcrum	Fighter	30-56	54-80	102-128
MiG-31	Fighter	-	-	24
Mirage F1	Fighter	?	?	?
Total	**Fighter**	**90-201**	**114-225**	**186-273**
F-4D Phantom	FGA	40-60	40-60	40-60
F-5E/F Tiger	FGA	45-68	45-68	45-68
Su-20	FGA	2-4?	2-4?	2-4?
Su-22M	FGA	35-40?	35-40?	35-40?
Su-24 Fencer	FGA	20-30	50-60	50-60
MiG-23BN Flogger	FGA	24?	24?	24?
MiG-27 Flogger	FGA	24?	24?	48?
Total	**FGA**	**190-250**	**220-280**	**244-304**
H-6D	Bomber	6?	6?	6?
Tu-22M Blinder	Bomber	4?	4?	12?
Total	**Bomber**	**10?**	**10?**	**18?**
Su-25 Frogfoot	Ground Attack	7?	7?	7?
Total combat air		**312?-468?**	**366-522**	**470-602**

Note: The Su-24 Fencer and MiG-29 totals include 24 and four (or eight), respectively, former Iraqi aircraft. Of the other aircraft that fled, it is assumed that the Russian aircraft have been incorporated but that some MiG-23s have been transferred to Sudan. The incorporated aircraft include 4 Su-20 Fitter C, 40 Su-22 Fitter H, 9-12 MiG-23 Floggers and 7 Su-25 Frogfoots. The 24 Mirage F1s have probably not been put into service. Iran has consistently claimed that only 22 aircraft fled Iraq in 1991 and that only this number, mostly civil airliners, may eventually be returned.[29]

Air defence has always been a problem, even in Imperial Iran. During the Iran-Iraq War, Iraqi aircraft roamed freely across Iranian skies and the Desert Storm experience made Iranian leaders concerned that the US or Israel could do the same to them. Iran has bought more advanced Surface to Air Missiles (SAM) from Russia but knows that it cannot defend all its airspace. Instead it has to hope to be able to defend point targets or to deter strikes by retaliating whether with Su-24s or with SSMs.[30]

Navy

The Iranian Navy and naval arm of the IRGC have been accorded a major role in Iran's post-war rearmament plans. This reflects Iran's view that the Gulf is its strategic lifeline and its perception that, since the late-1980s, the Gulf has virtually been turned into an American lake. Tehran recognises that control of the Gulf by a hostile power gives that power a stranglehold on its economic jugular by allowing disruption of its oil exports and its maritime trade routes. At the same time, Iran recognises that the ability to threaten GCC and international oil and gas export routes gives it considerable leverage in the region.

In response to this combination of threat and opportunity, Iran has adopted a strategy of naval guerrilla warfare. Understanding that it cannot compete with Western navies in respect of major surface platforms, Iran has concentrated on deploying small craft, mine warfare capabilities and anti-ship missiles.[31] These have been reinforced by the purchase of three Russian *Kilo*-class submarines, two of which have been deployed. Although not useable in most of the Gulf, these submarines can operate in the Gulf of Oman and Indian Ocean and are especially useful as minelayers. Three to five mini-submarines have also been purchased.[32] Acquisition has otherwise focused on small attack craft and patrol boats, including the Swedish *Boghammer* and the North Korean *Chehu*, in conjunction with shore-based anti-ship missiles. Ten *Hegu* fast attack craft have been delivered by China and are equipped with C-802 anti-ship missiles.[33] The HY-2 Silkworm was purchased from China and the SS-N-22 Sunburn from Ukraine. This acquisition trend is likely to continue so this study assumes an increase in Iranian holdings of small craft and missiles.

Naval Vessels

Type	1995	2000	2005 [34]
Destroyer	2-3	2-3	2-3
Frigate	3	3	3
Corvette	2	2	2
Missile Craft	10	10	15
Fast Attack Craft	71 [35]	76	85
Submarine	2	3	3
Midget Submarine	3-5	3-5	5
MCM	3	3	3
Amphibious craft	8	8	10
Armed Helicopters	9-16	9-16	9-16

Aside from their acquisition programme, Iran's naval forces have sought to improve their position to exert influence in the Gulf by spreading their forces across a number of islands and locations around the mouth of the Gulf. Missile batteries have been deployed at Bandar Abbas, Qeshm, Sirri and Abu Musa. Iranian positions on the disputed islands of Abu Musa and the Tunbs have been reinforced by the construction of an airport and a power station and the deployment of anti-aircraft defences. At the same time, Iranian naval forces have been engaged in an intensive cycle of exercises since 1994. These appear to have concentrated on offensive scenarios including landing marines, sabotaging oil platforms and ports, capturing ships and naval blockading.[36]

Although US officials often express concern at the growing capabilities of Iran's naval forces, their ability to project power across the Gulf remains limited. Its marine and commando force certainly can make hit-and-run raids on key installations but Iran has only limited lift capability. It has four Landing Ships (Tank) (LST) with a capacity of 225 troops and nine tanks and two or three LST with a capacity of 140 troops and eight tanks. It also has one or two further LST, a Landing Ship (Logistic), three Landing Craft (Tank) and 9-14 Landing Craft (Utility). It also has a number of logistics vessels which could support an amphibious operation. In total, these vessels give Iran the ability to project a maximum of up 1200 troops and 60 tanks in an amphibious landing. Such a force would be of limited utility in an opposed landing, especially in view of the GCC air threat it would face. A battlegroup-sized amphibious force could be inserted into a small Gulf state to support domestic rebels, but it would be only a token force and would remain highly vulnerable to being cut off from its supply lines.

Notes

1. A. Hashim, 'Iran's Military Situation,' in P. Clawson, ed., *Iran's Strategic Intentions and Capabilities* (Washington DC, National Defense University, 1994), pp. 153-219; A. Ehteshami, *After Khomeini: The Iranian Second Republic* (London, Routledge, 1995).
2. This section draws on my article 'Iran's Rearmament–How Great a Threat?' in *Jane's Intelligence Review* (hereafter *JIR*), July 1994, pp. 317-322. See also: S. Chubin, *Iran's National Security Policy* (Washington DC, Carnegie Endowment, 1994); M. Ziarati, 'Iranian national security policy,' *MEI*, 3 April 1992, pp. 18-19.
3. N. Schahgaldian, *The Iranian Military Under the Islamic Republic* (Santa Monica, RAND, 1987), pp. 17-49.
4. M. Eisenstadt, '*Déjà Vu* All Over Again? An Assessment of Iran's Military Buildup,' in Clawson, ed, *Iran's Strategic Intentions and Capabilities*, pp. 93-151. Ehteshami highlights Iranian claims that it no longer needs to import large quantities of arms since the imports before 1992 fulfilled its requirements. Ehteshami, *After Khomeini: The Iranian Second Republic*, p. 193.
5. A.H. Cordesman, *Iran & Iraq: The Threat from the Northern Gulf* (Boulder, CO, Westview Press, 1994), p. 39; SIPRI Yearbook 1995, *Armaments, Disarmament and International Security*, p. 494.

6. J. Bruce, 'Iran claims it is self-sufficient,' *Jane's Defence Weekly* (hereafter *JDW*), 14 October 1995, p. 21.
7. A. Ehteshami, 'Iran boosts domestic arms industry,' *International Defence Review* (hereafter *IDR)*, April 1994, pp. 72-73.
8. Schahgaldian, *The Iranian Military Under the Islamic Republic*, chapters IV and V; K. Katzman, *Iran's Revolutionary Guard Corps: Radical Ideology Despite Institutionalization in the Islamic Republic* (PhD Thesis, New York University, 1991).
9. J. Bruce, 'Iranian manoeuvres keep West on alert,' *Jane's Military Exercise & Training Monitor*, January–March 1996, p. 13.
10. On Iran's logistical problems, see: Schahgaldian, *The Iranian Military Under the Islamic Republic*, pp. 51-56.
11. Cordesman, *Iran & Iraq: The Threat from the Northern Gulf*, p. 47.
12. P. Beaver, ed, 'Iran,' *Jane's Sentinel Regional Security Assessment* (Coulsdon, Jane's Information Group, 1994), p. 21.
13. A. Ehteshami, 'Iran's National Strategy,' *IDR*, April 1994, pp. 29-37; R. Grimmett, *Iran: Conventional Arms Acquisitions* (Washington DC, Congressional Research Service, 22 February 1994); 'Iran's ongoing arms-buying spree,' *Washington Times*, 4 June 1992.
14. Thirty four had already been delivered. 'Poland Persists on Tank Sales,' *IHT*, 1995.
15. Ehteshami, 'Iran's National Strategy,' *IDR, op cit.*
16. Rathmell, 'Iran's Rearmament—How Great a Threat?' *JIR*; 'Iran,' *Jane's Sentinel Regional Security Assessment*, p. 17.
17. Ehteshami, 'Iran's National Strategy,' *IDR*; 'Iran's ongoing arms-buying spree,' *Washington Times*.
18. J. Bruce, 'Iran claims it has rebuilt and updated Iraqi MBTs,' *JDW*, 31 January 1996, p. 18.
19. 'Iran's ongoing arms-buying spree,' *Washington Times*.
20. 'Iran,' *Jane's Sentinel Regional Security Assessment*, p. 19.
21. 'Iran test-fires 122mm self-propelled gun,' *JDW*, 5 June 1996, p. 14.
22. Cordesman, *Iran & Iraq: The Threat from the Northern Gulf*, p. 48.
23. Ehteshami, 'Iran boosts domestic arms industry,' *IDR*, pp. 72-73.
24. J. Bruce, 'Iran's Air Force Seeks New Capabilities,' *Jane's Intelligence Review Pointer* (hereafter *JIR Pointer*), March 1995, p. 3. In addition, Iran claimed in 1995 that it had developed the capability to refuel its MiG-29s in the air, indicating a desire to build a long-range capability. J. Bruce, 'Iran extends 'Fulcrums' with airborne refuelling,' *JDW*, 26 August 1995, p. 16.
25. C. Van England, 'Iran Steps Up Arms Purchases to Prop Military,' *Christian Science Monitor*, 20 April 1992.

26. Tupolev, however, denied that it is supplying the Blinder. N. Friedman, 'Iranian Air Threat Emerging,' *Proceedings*, September 1992, pp. 123-4; Grimmett, *Iran: Conventional Arms Acquisitions*, p. 3.
27. Cordesman, *Iran & Iraq: The Threat from the Northern Gulf*, p. 55.
28. IISS notes that serviceability problems mean that some 50 per cent of US aircraft are probably unserviceable. The JCSS states that 60 per cent of Iran's aircraft are serviceable.
29. J. Bruce, 'Aircraft to stay as Iran and Iraq remain hostile,' *JDW*, 18 November 1995, p. 16; Ehteshami, 'Iran's National Strategy;' *IDR*; Cordesman, *Iran & Iraq: The Threat from the Northern Gulf*, p. 58.
30. A. Hashim, *The Crisis of the Iranian State*, Adelphi Paper 296 (London, IISS, 1995), p. 53.
31. Cordesman, *Iran & Iraq: The Threat from the Northern Gulf*, pp. 66-77.
32. Ehteshami, 'Iran's National Strategy,' *IDR, op cit.*
33. Grimmett, *Iran: Conventional Arms Acquisitions*, p. 4.
34. Assumes extra orders for small craft later this decade.
35. Includes IRGC craft.
36. J. Bruce, 'Choking the Strait,' *JIR*, September 1996, pp. 411-414.

CHAPTER 2
IRAQ

Since the Gulf War, Iraq has been rebuilding its armed forces in order both to confront external threats such as Iran and the Western-backed GCC states and to suppress domestic rebels in the north and the south of the country.[1] Although the debate continues over exactly how many losses the Iraqis suffered during the Gulf War, it is likely that the army ended the war and subsequent uprisings with as little as a quarter to a third of its pre-war divisional strength, a quarter of pre-war manpower and half of its equipment.[2]

The rebuilding has taken place against a background of political instability, with numerous senior officers losing their lives in coup attempts and purges.[3] In addition, it has been difficult to obtain new equipment or spare parts due to the UN embargo. Reorganisation and retraining programmes have been disrupted by operations against *Shi`ite* rebels in the south and the Kurds in the north.

Nonetheless, the Iraqi armed forces have been able to reconstitute a considerable portion of their pre-war combat power. Despite massive equipment losses, Iraq's military remains a potential threat to its neighbours. Once the country is again able to import modern hardware, spares and logistical support equipment, then its military will be a major force in the Gulf. This study however assumes that Iraq will not be able to begin importing arms before the year 2005.

Iraq's less than mighty military

In the run-up to Desert Storm, coalition intelligence analysts and outside observers overestimated the potency of the Iraqi military establishment. Analysts made two prime mistakes. First, they focused on front-line equipment holdings rather than on the intangibles of logistical infrastructures, doctrine, organisation and morale. Second, they took Iraq's performance in the war against Iran as a guide to Iraq's military effectiveness, rather than studying the

Iraq

more appropriate models of previous encounters between Western-style armed forces and modern Arab militaries.

In assessing the Iraqi military, analysts must be careful not to repeat these errors. Judged in terms of residual equipment holdings, manpower and Order of Battle (ORBAT), the Iraqi military still appears a potent force. In terms of operational effectiveness, however, the reality is somewhat different. As analyses of the Iraqi armed forces have shown, the Iraqi military did not perform well in the Iran-Iraq War. Although it became proficient at setpiece defensive operations it failed to develop an all round operational capability.[4]

During the war with Iran, several features of the Iraqi military became apparent which helped bring about its collapse in 1991 and which have prevented its re-emergence since. First, Iraq's massive arms build-up during the 1980s concentrated on front-line hardware. By the time of the 1988 ceasefire Iraq's army possessed up to 5700 MBTs, 3700 artillery tubes and an active manpower of some 800 000 organised into at least 60 division equivalents. This front-line strength was not, however, backed up by a supporting infrastructure. Throughout the 1980s Iraq relied on imports of military consumables from around the world to keep its forces operational.

Arms imports averaged between $3 and $5 billion per year during the war and Iraq generally relied on replacing rather than repairing its hardware. The domestic arms industry was adept at re-engineering equipment but supplied few of the military's basic needs. This weakness in its defence-industrial base has meant that, since UN sanctions were imposed in 1990, the Iraqi army has suffered a steady degradation in its equipment operability and operational capabilities.[5] Although by 1993 Iraq had rebuilt some 80 per cent of its military-industrial base, the capabilities of this base remained limited.[6] Its manufacturing plants have been active in refurbishing tanks and aircraft and can also supply explosives, fuses, defence electronics and vehicle parts. Assembly of T-72 MBTs has reportedly restarted. Nonetheless, there has been a great deal of cannibalisation from existing equipment to keep vehicles running.

Second, the army has consistently operated with a hollow organisational structure. Its large numbers of divisions have never been fully rounded out. Divisional structures were often intended to be filled out by reservists or additional conscripts in time of crisis but, as the coalition victory showed, the quality and dedication of many of these men was not very high. As a consequence of the equipment losses in 1991, even Iraq's reduced number of divisions cannot fill their mandated equipment holdings.

The third factor relates to Iraq's command structure and operational doctrine. Here it is hard to separate political and military factors. Saddam's exceptionally centralised and brutal form of autocracy is not conducive to encouraging the devolution of command and display of initiative that is so highly prized in modern military doctrine. Since the Second Gulf War Saddam has tightened even further his personal grip over the armed forces. This process may be politically necessary to keep the regime in power but it has hampered the ability of the general staff to improve the army's military performance.[7]

This politically-inspired inability to adopt new doctrines or devolve command feeds through into operations and training. During the Iran-Iraq War the army became adept at positional defence and adequate at set-piece, heavy artillery assaults. Anything more than this was however largely beyond it. Since 1991 the army has been retraining but it lacks the ability to mount combined arms operations, operate at divisional level or conduct manoeuvre warfare.[8]

Related to this inability to achieve inter-arm coordination was a failure to deploy airpower effectively. A great deal was spent on buying modern aircraft but these were never used to best advantage. Again, Iraq concentrated on acquiring large quantities of the latest equipment, a strategy which led to problems with sustainability, training and interoperability. At the time of Desert Storm at least a third of all aircraft were probably unserviceable. In terms of doctrine, the Air Force never developed an integrated warfighting strategy. Against Iran, Iraq's strike aircraft were used in penny packets. They had little experience of operating against a functional Third World, let alone a Western, air force.

Post-war rebuilding

There have been few indications that these systemic problems have been addressed since 1991. The state of Iraqi politics and the country's isolation will probably make it impossible to do so in the short term. Instead, Iraq's high command has got on with the more immediate task of reconstituting some of the military's strength and seeing to immediate security needs.[9]

The army has been the prime focus of effort.[10] The uprisings which followed the retreat from Kuwait almost shattered the army as numerous units went over to the rebels but the better-armed and disciplined loyalist units won out in the end. The approach since 1991 has been to reduce the numbers of formations and personnel, amalgamate units and concentrate on rebuilding armoured and mechanised units. In 1991 the army was infantry-heavy but it now has a greater proportion of armoured and mechanised formations. The regular army now has two or three armoured divisions and three mechanised divisions out of a total of 20-23 divisions.[11]

These divisions are, at least nominally, structured along the following lines: armoured divisions have two armoured brigades and one mechanised brigade; mechanised divisions have two mechanised and one armoured brigade; infantry divisions have three infantry brigades and one tank battalion. Armoured brigades have three armoured and one mechanised battalion while mechanised brigades have three mechanised and one tank battalion. Divisions usually have four artillery battalions in support. These regular units are generally equipped with BTR family APCs and older Soviet tanks such as the T-55 and T-62. An unknown number of the T-55s were upgraded before 1991 with the T-72 125mm gun while others have *appliqué* armour.

The Republican Guard developed from a small unit tasked to protect the President and the capital. During the latter years of the Iran-Iraq War it grew to eight divisions as well as numerous independent brigades, adding perhaps another four division equivalents. The expansion of the force diluted its status as the praetorian guard of the regime, but the Republican Guards had become by 1990 the best-equipped and paid units. They were used as heavy formations and Republican Guard tank battalions had nine more tanks than regular army formations. They tended to get the best equipment, such as T-72 MBTs, BMP AIFVs, French GCT self-propelled howitzers and Austrian GHN-45 towed howitzers.

Since the Gulf War, the regime has concentrated its energies on reconstituting the Guard formations and has rebuilt eight divisions. There are three armoured divisions (al-Nida, al-Hammurabi and al-Medina), one mechanised division (al-Abid) and four infantry divisions (al-Adnan, al-Nebuchadnezzar, al-Baghdad and one other). These units are, however, undermanned and underequipped. According to standard Iraqi ORBATs, the total manpower of these eight divisions should be 112 400 whereas in fact they probably only have up to 80 000 soldiers. Likewise, MBT holdings should be 1320, against a likely actual figure of no more than 800 APC and AIFV holdings should be 2260, against a probable actual figure of up to 1100.[12]

The Republican Guards' status as the protector of the regime has also been undermined with the expansion since 1991 of the Presidential Guard Force. This 8000-14 000 strong armoured unit is based in Baghdad.

Iraq

MBT

Type	Role	1995	2000	2005
T-62/72	MBT	400	400	400
T-54/55/M-77 Type 59/-69	MBT	500	500	500
Assorted	MBT	?	?	?
Total	MBT	2000-2700	2000-2700	2000-2700

Assorted MBTs include Chieftain Mk3/5, M-47/8 and M-60A1.

Note: During the Gulf War the operability of Iraqi MBTs was questionable since they were used in static posts. The lack of spares and cannibalisation since 1990 has reduced reliability further. The IISS judges that most of the US and British tanks are inoperable. NATO appears to estimate that 60 per cent of the older Soviet, US and British MBTs are non-operational.[13]

ARV/AIFV/APC

Type	Role	1995	2000	2005
Assorted Total	ARV	1500	1500	1500
BMP-1	AIFV	70?	70?	70?
BMP-2	AIFV	?	?	?
Total	AIFV	900	900	900
Assorted Total	APC	2000	2000	?

Assorted ARV include: PT-76, EE-9 Cascavel, BRDM-2, EE-3 Jararaca, AML-60/90.
Assorted APC include: BTR-152, BTR-50/60, M-113A1/A2, OT-62/64, MTLB, YW-531, Panhard M-3, EE11 Urutu, Walid, BMD-1.

Surface to Surface Missiles

Type	Role	1995	2000	2005
SS-1 Scud B/C	SSM	16?[14]	?	?

Artillery

Type	Role	1995	2000	2005
FROG-7, Laith 90	SSR	?	?	?
Total	SSM	16?	?	?
Assorted Total	SP Artillery	230?	230?	230?
Assorted Total	Towed Artillery	1500?	1500?	1500?
Assorted Total	MRL	250?	250?	250?
Assorted Total	Mortar	?	?	?

Assorted SP artillery include: 240mm 2S4, 210mm Fao, 155mm M109A1/A2, 155mm Majnoon, 152mm 2S3.

Assorted towed artillery include: 180mm S-23, 155mm G5, 155mm GH N-45, 155mm M-114, 152mm D-1, 152mm 2A36, 152mm M1937, 130mm M-46, 130mm Type 59, 122mm D-74, 122mm D-30, 122mm M1938, 105mm M-56 pack.

Assorted MRL include: 300mm Sajil 60, 262mm Ababil, 240mm Nasr, 132mm BM-13/16, 127mm Astros II, 122mm BM-21, 122mm BM-11, 108mm FGT, 107mm MRS.

Assorted mortars include: 240mm, 160mm M-1943, 120mm, 81mm.

Anti-Tank Weapons

Type	Role	1995	2000	2005
Assorted Total	AT Gun (towed)	?	?	?
Assorted Total	RCL	?	?	?
Assorted Total	ATGW	1500?	1500?	1500?

Assorted AT guns include: 100mm, 85mm.
Assorted RCL include: 107mm, 82mm B-10, 73mm SPG-9.
Assorted ATGW include: AT-3 *Sagger*, AT-4 *Spigot*, SS-11, Milan, HOT.

The other major element in the army's ORBAT is its helicopters. Helicopter gunships proved a potent weapon in the war against Iran and in operations against the Kurds. The army air corps deployed about 160 in 1990, including up to 45 Mi-24 Hinds, SA-342 Gazelles, BO-105s and Alouettes. Perhaps 120 remain in service and they have been used extensively against *Shi'ite* villages and guerillas in the south. This intensive use and the lack of spares, however, means that serviceability is poor, with perhaps only 80 being fully operational.[15]

Army Aviation
(Armed only)

Type	Role	1995	2000	2005
Bo-105	Attack Helo	10-75?	10-75?	10-75?
Mi-24	Attack Helo	?	?	?
Mi-25	Attack Helo	12-30?	12-30?	12-30?
SA-316	Attack Helo	5?	5?	5?
SA-319	Attack Helo	20?	20?	20?
SA-321	Attack Helo	7?	7?	7?
SA-342 Gazelle	Attack Helo	20-50?	20-50?	20-50?
Total	**Attack Helo**	**64-185**	**64-185**	**64-185?**

Air Force

Before Desert Storm, the Iraqi Air Force was a powerful entity, at least on paper, with almost 800 fixed wing combat aircraft.[16] Some 470 of these were older types such as MiG-15/19/21s, Su-7/20/22s, F-6/7s and Hunters but Iraq had acquired a stock of modern platforms. These included 65 Mirage F-1s (various versions), 50 MiG-23BNs, 22 MiG-25 interceptors, 48 Su-24 Fencers, 48 MiG-29 Fulcrum B/Cs, MiG 27s, Tu-22 Blinders and Tu-16 Badgers.

The performance of these aircraft was especially noteworthy since they were configured to employ a wide range of systems and ordnance. The Su-24Ds were equipped with refuelling probes, electronic warfare suites and could use laser guided munitions. The Mirages had Exocet anti-ship missiles as well as AS-14 Kedge AGMs and AS-30L laser guided bombs.

The Air Force had also begun to rectify some of the operational problems it had recognised during the war with Iran, for instance developing the *Adnan* Airborne Early Warning aircraft based on the IL-76 Candid. Iraq's fighters were in the early stages of netting in to a modern Command, Control, Communications and Intelligence (C^3I) system when Desert Storm dealt a body blow to the Air Force.[17]

During the war, Iraq lost about half of its aircraft and was dealt a further blow when Iran announced in 1992 that it would appropriate the 132 Iraqi jets which had taken refuge inside Iran during the conflict. Some of the remaining combat aircraft are high quality but serviceability is a major problem. Flight training and operations did not begin again until 1992, when missions were flown against *Shi'ite* rebel targets in the south, and are still constrained by the No-Fly Zones in the north and south of the country. Before sanctions were imposed, the Air Force relied heavily on Russian and French technical assistance to keep its aircraft in the air, but as time has gone on the absence of this help has degraded operational capabilities.[18]

Iraq's air defence system on the eve of Desert Storm was also formidable. Since the embarrassment of Israel's successful raid on the Osirak nuclear reactor in 1981, the Air Force and Army had put in place an extensive umbrella that covered the country's key assets. The C^3 system, called KARI, was supplied by France and netted in radars, missiles and guns across the country. This system was combined with the Soviet doctrine of a layered defensive network. At the start of the war against the coalition, Iraq had some 550 SAMs and 380 Anti-Aircraft Artillery sites around Baghdad alone, making it better defended than any city in East Europe against which NATO expected to operate during the Cold War.[19]

This centralised network was dismantled by the American-led air onslaught. About half the command centres were destroyed, along with perhaps a third of the fixed-site SAMs. The network has suffered further damage since, particularly on occasions when SAM batteries have been engaged by USAF aircraft patrolling the No Fly Zones, such as in the south in January 1993. Without a massive influx of new equipment and funds to rebuild the system, Iraq's air defences will be no match for the types of advanced strike aircraft now being deployed by its neighbours, notably Iran's Su-24s and Saudi Arabia's F-15XPs and Tornado IDS.

Combat Aircraft[20]

Type	Role	1995	2000	2005
F-7	Fighter	40?	40?	40?
MiG-21	Fighter	30-110?	30-110?	30-110?
MiG-23 Flogger	Fighter	25-40?	25-40?	25-40?
MiG-25 Foxbat	Fighter	6-20?	6-20?	6-20?
Mirage F-1EQ	Fighter	20?	20?	20?
MiG-29	Fighter	6-15?	6-15?	6-15?
Total	Fighter	127-245	127-245	127-245
SU-24	FGA	?	?	?
MiG-23BN	FGA	40?	40?	40?
Mirage F-1EQ5	FGA	40?	40?	40?
Su-7	FGA	5?	5?	5?
Su-20/22	FGA	55?	55?	55?
Su-25	FGA	30?	30?	30?
Total	FGA	130-170	130-170	130-170
H-6D	Bomber	1-3	1-3	1-3
Tu-22	Bomber	2-4	2-4	2-4
Total	Bomber	3-7	3-7	3-7
Total combat air		260-422	260-422	260-422

Navy

Iraq's navy has never been a significant force in the Gulf and is likely to remain marginal for some time to come. Although it carried out a number of small raids and minelaying operations during the Gulf

War, it was virtually destroyed by coalition and air forces. It now has only one frigate, the *Ibn Marjid/Khaldun* used for training and a handful of small missile and fast attack craft. These include one or two Soviet *Osa* class craft.

Before the Iran-Iraq War, Iraq had initiated plans to expand its navy so as to be able to challenge Iran. It ordered four frigates, six corvettes, a replenishment ship, a dry dock and naval helicopters from Italy. Deployment of these vessels would have turned the Iraqi navy into a significant force. Their delivery was halted by an Italian arms embargo during the Iran-Iraq War and there was no time to resume the order before the Gulf War broke out.[21]

Naval Vessels

Type	1995	2000	2005
Frigate	1	1	1
Missile Craft	1-2	1-2	1-2
Fast Attack Craft	7	7	7
MCM	4	4	4

The 1981 Italian order shows that the Iraqi navy has the ambition of deploying a potent naval force able to challenge Iranian control of the sealanes. For the foreseeable future, though, Iraq's navy will not count for anything in the regional strategic balance.

Notes

1. This section draws on my article: 'Iraq's Military–Waiting for Change,' *JIR*, Vol. 7 No. 2 , pp. 76-80.
2. For discussions of Iraqi losses in the conflict, see: J.G. Heidenrich, 'The Gulf War: How Many Iraqis Died?' *Foreign Policy*, No. 91 (Spring 1993), pp. 108-125 and discussion in the journal's Letters section, *Foreign Policy*, No. 91, (Summer 1993), pp. 182-192.
3. 'Saddam: Buying Time,' *JDW*, 13 July 1991, pp. 61-63.
4. E. Karsh, *The Iran-Iraq War: A Military Analysis*, Adelphi Paper 220 (London, IISS, 1987); S.C. Pelletiere and D.V. Johnson II, *Lessons Learned: the Iran-Iraq War* (Carlisle Barracks, PA, US Army War College, Strategic

Studies Institute, 1991); A.H Cordesman and A.R. Wagner, *The Lessons of Modern War,* Vol. 2, *The Iran-Iraq War* (London, Mansell, 1990).
5. 'Iraq's shrinking army needs guns,' *Foreign Report,* 8 November 1994.
6. US Congress, *Iraq's Nuclear Weapons Capability and IAEA Inspections in Iraq,* Hearing before House Committee on Foreign Affairs, 29 June 1993.
7. Cordesman, *Iran and Iraq: The Threat from the Northern Gulf,* pp.201-202.
8. 'Iraqi Maneuvers Are First Since War,' *IHT,* 31 October 1992
9. Cordesman, *Iran and Iraq: The Threat from the Northern Gulf,* pp. 187-199.
10. M. Eisenstadt, *Like a Phoenix from the Ashes: The Future of Iraqi Military Power,* Policy Paper 36 (Washington DC, Washington Institute for Near East Policy, 1993), pp. 47-52.
11. M. Eisenstadt, 'The Iraqi Armed Forces Two Years On,' *JIR,* March 1993, pp. 121-127; 'West takes tally of Saddam's might,' *JDW,* 8 August 1992.
12. Cordesman, *Iran and Iraq: The Threat from the Northern Gulf,* pp.199-200.
13. Private discussion with NATO officials, January 1996.
14. Author's private discussions with UN officials in November 1995; UN Security Council, *Report of the Secretary-General on the activities of the Special Comission established by the Secretary-General pursuant to paragraph 9 (b) (i) of resolution 687 (1991),* 11 April 1996, p. 12. See also D. Isby, 'Iraq's Residual Scud Force,' *JIR,* Vol 7, No 3, pp. 115-117.
15. The IISS says the serviceability of rotary wing aircraft is 'poor'.
16. Eisenstadt, *Like a Phoenix from the Ashes: The Future of Iraqi Military Power,* pp. 53-57.
17. M. Gaines, 'Paper Tigers?' *Flight International,* 9-15 January 1991, pp. 20-22; D. Eshel, 'The Iraqi Air Force—How Effective Is It,' *Military Technology,* February 1991, pp. 72-3.
18. Cordesman, *Iran and Iraq: The Threat from the Northern Gulf,* pp. 214-219.
19. M.R. Gordon and General B.E. Trainor, *The Generals' War* (Boston: Little, Brown and Company, 1995), pp. 102-122; 'Success from the air,' *JDW,* 6 April 1991; D. Ball, *The Intelligence War in the Gulf* (Canberra: Strategic and Defence Studies Centre, Australian National University, 1991), pp. 68-70.
20. IISS says the serviceability of fixed wing aircraft is good, but Jane's *Sentinel* suggests that the numbers of operational aircraft are much lower.
21. Cordesman, *Iran and Iraq: The Threat from the Northern Gulf,* pp. 220-224.

CHAPTER 3
SAUDI ARABIA

Saudi Arabia regards itself as being surrounded by rival and potentially hostile powers. Its defence forces must therefore face in all directions. The Kingdom is bordered on the north by Iraq. Even if the current Iraqi regime is replaced in the near term, the Kingdom will have to regard Iraq as a potential threat. In terms of capabilities, Iraq has demonstrated the ability to mobilise large armed forces and has developed a range of military industries. In terms of intentions, it is likely that future Iraqi regimes will want to revise the post-Gulf War correlation of forces and to challenge the Kingdom's leading regional role as well as the post-war border settlement with Kuwait. To the north-west, Saudi Arabia is bordered by Jordan. Although Jordan is militarily weak, traditional rivalries between the Hashemite and the Al Saud mean that the Saudis watch nervously for any sign of Hashemite revanchism.

To the south, the Kingdom is nervous of Yemen which has a large population and an experienced, if shrinking, army.[1] Although Yemen will remain impoverished and militarily under-equipped for some time yet, long-standing rivalries and an unresolved border dispute mean that Saudi leaders regard it as a potential threat.

To the east, the Kingdom sees Iran as a rival both in geopolitical and in religious terms. Although Saudi-Iranian tensions have eased since the 1980s there are tensions over the *Hajj* and Riyadh remains concerned at Iranian attempts to exploit Shia discontent in its eastern province and in Bahrain. To the west, the Kingdom's Red Sea coast has seen tremendous growth, especially as the Iran-Iraq War encouraged the shift of economic, oil and transport projects to the Red Sea coast. Over the past decade, the Kingdom has come to see the Red Sea as its second vital waterway, after the Gulf. Iranian links with Sudan and Sudan's support for radical Islamist groups concern the Kingdom, as does instability in the Horn of Africa.

Saudi Arabia

In defence terms, the Kingdom faces a fundamental geostrategic dilemma. It has a large land area, 2.15 million sq km, but limited manpower, some 18.6 million.[2] Although the state was a revisionist power early this century, when it extended its control over the bulk of the Arabian Peninsula, it is now a *status quo* power determined to protect its territorial and economic gains. Its key asset is its oil wealth. This has enabled it to provide for its security against foreign threats in three ways. First, by building a close alliance with the US. Second, by using its wealth to reward friends and buy off enemies. Third, by building a modern and lavishly-equipped military establishment.[3]

Over the past quarter of a century, Saudi Arabia's forces have been transformed from light mechanised units into a powerful modern army and air force, deploying large quantities of the latest technology and supported by an extensive logistic infrastructure.[4] This 'brute force' building effort of the forces has cost perhaps $250bn over the past decade alone.[5] In order to counter threats from all sides, Saudi Arabia had to develop logistical infrastructures facing in all directions—the King Abdul Aziz Military City facing Yemen, the King Fahd Military City facing Jordan and the King Khalid Military City facing Iraq.[6] In addition, naval bases have been built on both coasts and airbases at numerous locations across the country. The annual cost of maintaining this military machine has been put at $15 billion.[7]

In the wake of reviews of its defence needs conducted after the Gulf War, Saudi Arabia has been engaged in further expansion plans and arms purchases. Despite a fall in oil revenues, Riyadh is determined to fulfill its expansion plans.[8] Its air force, already established as the most effective air defence force in the Gulf, is developing an offensive capability. The ground forces are being expanded and trying to become proficient at manouevre warfare. The navy is being built up into a two fleet force.

Ground Forces

Saudi Arabia's army has expanded rapidly, from some 40 000 men in the late 1980s to around 70 000 in the mid-1990s. The current force structure, three armoured brigades, five mechanised brigades, one airborne brigade, a Royal Guard brigade, eight artillery battalions and an aviation element, would however need around 100 000 to be fully manned. Units are undermanned by an average of about 20-30 per cent.[9]

This manpower shortage will be more pressing if proposed expansion plans go ahead. A US-Saudi joint review, the Malcor Report, carried out in August 1991, reportedly called for the creation of between seven and nine divisions. Cordesman, however, estimates that the army actually has more modest plans to add an armoured and a mechanised brigade and to convert from a brigade to a divisional command structure. This would involve the creation of three divisions in the north facing Iraq, one division in the south and one in the centre of the country. Combat personnel would increase to 70 000, from 37 500 in 1993 and total army manpower would increase to perhaps 120 000.[10]

Saudi Arabia's other ground force is the Saudi Arabian National Guard (SANG). This is a tribally-based force with mainly an internal security role.[11] It did, however, fight creditably against the Iraqis at Khafji in 1991 and its commander, Crown Prince Abdullah, is keen to expand and upgrade it. Modernisation of the SANG has proceeded over the past decade, with assistance from an official American team, the Office of the Project Manager (OPM) and the Vinnel Corporation. The Imam Muhammad bin Saud mechanised brigade was formed in the early 1980s and the King Abdul Aziz brigade in 1985. SANG was expanded after the Gulf War and now has around 30 000 actives in combat units, perhaps 15 000 to 30 000 part time guardsmen in internal security units and tribal levies numbering perhaps 15 000. In addition to its two mechanised brigades it has between four and six lorried infantry brigades which serve as local area security forces.[12]

The SANG is re-equipping with Light Armoured Vehicles (LAV) to replace its V-150 Commando wheeled AIFVs. It is becoming a heavier force with the acquisition of armoured mortars and LAV assault guns. However, ambitious plans to turn it into an armoured force are unlikely to be fulfilled for political reasons. It is likely to remain a mechanised infantry force. Reports suggest that the SANG's advisers have studied plans to expand it into a force of up to 100 000 men, organised in three heavy mechanised or armoured brigades, but this would not be implemented until the late 1990s at the earliest.[13]

The army and SANG's modernisation and expansion plans are backed by a large-scale equipment acquisition effort. Some purchases have been delayed for fiscal reasons, but overall the ground forces' holdings of modern equipment are set to increase markedly over the coming decade.

MBT

Type	Role	1995	2000	2005
Abrams M-1A2	MBT	315	550	700
M-60A3	MBT	400-450	400-450	400-450
AMX-30	MBT	290-300[14]	145	-
Total	MBT	1005-1065	1005-1145	1100-1150

The army intends to phase out its obsolete AMX-30s, possibly by the end of the decade. All M60A1s have now been upgraded to A3 standard and are a match for T-72s and T-80s. 315 M-1A2s were ordered in September 1989 and are now in service. In 1990 a further 235 were ordered but delivery was postponed in July 1992. Reports indicate that the army plans to deploy 700 M-1A2s eventually but the exact numbers are unclear and the Kingdom may opt for Giat Leclerc or Vickers Desert Challenger MBTs instead of the extra Abrams.[15] This study assumes that 235 M1A2s are delivered this decade and half of the AMX-30s are phased out, the remaining AMX-30s are phased out by 2005 and an additional 150 M1A2s are bought.[16]

ARV/AIFV/APC

Type	Role	1995	2000	2005
AML-60/90	ARV	200-280	200-280	200-280
Panhard M3	ARV	150	150	150
Total	**ARV**	**350-430**	**350-430**	**350-430**
M-2 *Bradley*	AIFV	400	550	700
AMX-10P	AIFV	490-570+	490-570+	490-570+
LAV-25 (SANG)	AIFV	262	800[17]	1044
V-150 *Commando* (SANG)	AIFV	980-1100	980[18]	900
Piranha (SANG)	AIFV	65	65	65
Total	**AIFV**	**2197-2332**	**2885-2965**	**3199-3279**
M-113	APC	1000-700	1000-1700	1000-1700
Total	**APC**	**1000-1700**	**1000-1700**	**1000-1700**

The army is keen to standardise its wide array of AIFV/APCs by focusing on the M2 Bradley and the M113 APC. In 1988 the Kingdom ordered 110 Bradleys and in 1990 it ordered a further 200. Cordesman suggests that the Saudis may seek to buy a total of 550-700 Bradleys and try to equip the remainder of their mechanised troops with M113s.[19] This study assumes that 550 Bradleys are deployed by 2000 and 700 by 2005. The SANG has ordered 1117 LAVs. It is not clear, though, if these will replace the V-150s or whether the latter will be handed over to its infantry units. The LAV order includes 384 LAV-25s equipped with 25mm chain guns, 111 LAV-ATs armed with TOW ATGW, 182 command vehicles, 130 LAV assault guns, probably with 90mm gun turrets and 71

Saudi Arabia

ambulances. Seventy three of the LAVs will be equipped with 120mm mortars and so are counted under artillery holdings.[20]

Artillery

Type	Role	1995	2000	2005
CSS-2	SSM	8-12 (30-50 msl)	8-12 (30-50 msl)	8-12 (30-50 msl)
Total	**SSM**	**8-12 (30-50 msl)**	**8-12 (30-50 msl)**	**8-12 (30-50 msl)**
155mm M-109A1B/A2	SP How	100-220	100-220	100-220
155mm GCT	SP How	50-90	50-90	50-90
Total	**SP Artillery**	**150-310**	**150-310**	**150-310**
203mm M-115	How (towed)	8-115 (in store)	8-115 (in store)	-
155mm FH-70	How (towed)	40-72 (in store)	40-72 (in store)	-
155mm M-198/M-114	How (towed)	50-140	50-140	50-140
105mm M-101	How (towed)	20-100 (in store)	20-100 (in store)	-
155mm M-198 (SANG)	How (towed)	30	30	30
105mm M102 (SANG)	How (towed)	30-40	30-40	30-40
Total	**Towed Artillery**	**110-210 (+68-287 in store)**	**110-210 (+68-287 in store)**	**110-210**[21]
Astros II	MRL	60	70	90

41

MLRS	MRL	-	-	9
Total	MRL	60	70	99
120mm Brandt	Mortar	48	48	-22
120mm LAV (SANG)	SP Mortar	-	73	73
107mm 4.2in M-30	SP Mortar	150	150	150
81mm M125A	SP Mortar	70	70	70
V150/M163 (SANG)	SP Mortar	20	70	70
Total	Mortar	288	411	363

In 1990 Saudi Arabia ordered 9 MLRS systems, including 2880 rockets, nine MV-755A2 command post carriers and communication equipment. In 1991, however, the Kingdom postponed the order for a number of years due to the high costs involved.[23] This study assumes that the nine MLRS are purchased by 2005. It also assumes that previously announced plans to purchase more ASTROS systems go ahead.

During the Gulf War, Saudi artillery demonstrated limited ability in manouevre and combined arms warfare. It had little ability in counter battery fire or to coordinate fire plans. Towards the end of this decade it may reduce these problems with the integration of new fire control and target acquisition systems.[24]

Saudi Arabia has a good stock of anti-tank weapons, many mounted on mobile platforms and plentifully supplied with spare rounds.

Anti-Tank Weapons

Saudi Arabia

Type	Role	1995	2000	2005
106mm M-40A1	RCL	50?	50?	50?
90mm M-67	RCL	100?	100?	100?
84mm Carl Gustav	RCL	300-400	300-400	300-400
Total	**RCL**	**300-550**	**300-550**	**300-550**
TOW-2 (inc SP on VCC-1, M-113A and other)	ATGW	200-950	200-950	200-950
M-47 Dragon	ATGW	1000?	1000?	1000?
HOT (inc AMX-10P SP)	ATGW	90-100	90-100	90-100
Total	**ATGW**	**290-2050**	**290-2050**	**290-2050**

Army Aviation
(Armed only)

Type	Role	1995	2000	2005
Bell 406CS	Attack Helo	15	15	15
AH-64 Apache	Attack Helo	12	12	36
Total	**Attack Helo**	**27**	**27**	**51**

When it ordered a dozen Apaches in September 1990, Saudi Arabia made plain its interest in buying a total of 48 Apaches, as well as further attack helicopters from European suppliers. The Saudis have experienced problems with operating and maintaining the Apaches but their interest in building heli-mobile forces is evident. This study assumes that 24 extra Apaches are acquired by 2005.[25]

The Saudi army's logistics set up is outstanding among developing nations. It has acquired large numbers of tank transporters, service and support vehicles, spare parts and ammunition. The ability of its military infrastructure to support coalition forces in 1990-1 was an indication of the investment it has put into its logistical framework.[26] For the near term, however, the army and the SANG are reliant on foreign contractor support. During the Gulf War contractors often deployed into the field along with Saudi forces. This procedure appears to have worked adequately, but the Saudis recognise the need to train and deploy indigenous support personnel.[27]

Air Force

The Royal Saudi Air Force (RSAF) has been the focus of Saudi efforts as it is the only arm capable of deploying rapidly to face threats from any direction and it is cash and technology rather than manpower intensive. During the 1980s, the RSAF developed into a capable defensive force. It gained a lot of experience at counter-air missions, though admittedly with close help and even supervision from the USAF. Its main strength is in its five interceptor squadrons with F-15C/Ds and four FGA squadrons with Tornado IDS and F-5E. These are supported by five AWACS and a tanker squadron. In addition, the RSAF enjoys the use of lavishly equipped and protected airbases as well as advanced munitions. The country is increasingly well protected by the RSAF's and the Air Defence Force's radar and missile defence net, under the Peace Shield programme.[28]

The RSAF is now acquiring American F-15XPs and British Tornado IDS. These will, by the end of the decade, give it four more strike squadrons which will give it an unprecedented ability to hit targets deep inside Iran, Iraq or any other adversary. This potential ability will be constrained by the lack of an ability to plan and conduct large scale attack missions. The RSAF will have to integrate closely with the USAF for such missions.[29] Cordesman estimates that it will be at least 'ten years [from 1993] before the RSAF can adequately match its offensive and defensive capabilities. It will need at least a decade more ... to become an effective air force capable of force-on-force operations and combined operations.'[30]

Saudi Arabia

Of the 72 F-15XPs the US agreed in 1992 to supply, 24 will be air defence versions and the remainder strike variants. The purchase totals some $9bn and they will be delivered at the rate of one squadron a year from 1995. The first full squadron should be operational by mid-1996 and the final delivery will be in 1998. By 1999, when the aircraft are absorbed, the F-5s will be phased out and it is likely they will not be replaced. In addition, under *al-Yamamah II* Saudi Arabia is purchasing 48 Tornado IDS/GR1 as part of a deal worth $7.5bn (having found the ADV inadequate it has converted most of its ADV to strike and reconnaissance tasks). A letter of intent was signed in 1988 and the sale finalised in February 1993. It includes shelters, maintenance, training and weapons. Forty Hawk trainers and 20 Hawk strike aircraft are included.[31] The only likely future orders are for more training aircraft, perhaps additional Hawks to replace the F-5s.

Combat Aircraft

Type	Role	1995	2000	2005
F-15C *Eagle*	Fighter	70-78	70-78	70-78
F-15D	Fighter	20-21	20-21	20-21
F-15XP/ADV	Fighter	-	24	24
Tornado ADV	Fighter	22-24	22-24	22-24
Total	Fighter	**113-122**	**136-147**	**136-147**
F-5E Tiger II	FGA	43-56	-	-
F-5F	FGA	14	-	-
F-15XP strike	Strike	-	48	48
Hawk	FGA	-	20	20
Tornado IDS	Strike	42-47	42-47	90-95
Total	FGA/ strike	**132-142**	**110-115**	**158-163**
RF-5E	Recce	8-10	-	-
Total combat air		**253-274**	**246-262**	**294-310**

For the purposes of this study, it is assumed that the F-15XPs and Hawks will be operational by the year 2000 but that the additional Tornadoes will not be in service until early next decade. By 2000, assuming all the contracts are fulfilled, the RSAF will have an additional 24 fighters, 48 strike and 20 light strike aircraft. Over the same period, it will probably phase all of its F-5s out of operational roles. The total number of aircraft will remain similar to that at present but the quality will have increased dramatically. By the year 2005, an extra 48 strike aircraft will be in the inventory, bringing the RSAF's total combat air up to around 300 platforms.

In modern air warfare the number and quality of platforms is only one component. The RSAF has also invested heavily in weapons systems and C^3I assets. Its air-to-air munitions include various versions of the AIM-9 Sidewinder and AIM-7F Sparrow. Air-to-ground munitions include the AGM-65 Maverick, AS-15, AS-30 and ALARM anti-radar missile. Its air interception screen is controlled by five E-3A AWACS and the Kingdom is considering buying four more to achieve comprehensive coverage of its northern border. In order to make best use of its equipment, the RSAF is now focusing on acquiring the equipment necessary to make best use of its platforms and weapons, for instance mission planning packages. The development of an offensive stance will also require improved reconnaissance assets.[32]

Navy

Saudi Arabia's Navy has undergone dramatic expansion over the last decade but is not yet able to operate on its own. Its two fleets are based at Jeddah and Jubail, but Saudi vessels are notoriously reluctant to operate out of coastal waters. Although originally equipped by the US, in the 1980s the Kingdom turned to France to supply its major naval requirements. Under the *Sawari I* programme it purchased four F-2000 frigates as well as patrol boats and naval helicopters.

The Saudi Navy placed tentative orders during the Gulf War for three French Lafayette F-3000 frigates. It is assumed that these will be in service just after the turn of the century. It has ordered three more *Sandown* class Mine Counter Measures Vessels, known as *al-Jawf*. The first was delivered in December 1995 and the other two will be in service by the end of the decade.[33]

Type	1995	2000	2005
Frigate	8	8	11
Missile Craft	9	9	9
Fast Attack Craft	20	20	20
MCM	8	10	10
Armed Helicopters	20-23	20-23	25

The Saudi Navy is fairly well equipped with platforms, weapons and helicopters. It enjoys extensive logistical back up at its well-equipped bases and has invested heavily in automated logistics and command and control systems. Nonetheless, observers judge that it will be many years before it is able to operate without close support from its Western allies.[34]

Notes

1. Yemen has cut its armed forces by some 50 000 men since the 1994 Civil War. R. Scott, 'In Sanaa: Arms and the Man,' *The Middle East*, July/August 1995, pp. 5-7.
2. This figure may be an overestimate and in any case only some 12.5 million are Saudi nationals.
3. P. Wilson and G. Graham, Saudi Arabia: *The Coming Storm* (Armank, NY, M.E. Sharpe, 1994), p. 140-170; N. Safran, *Saudi Arabia: The Ceaseless Quest for Security* (Cambridge, MA, Belknap Press, 1985).
4. H. Krech, 'Die Modernisierung der saudiarabischen Streitkraefte,' *Europäische Sicherheit*, April 1994, pp. 177-178.
5. As Cordesman notes, much of Saudi Arabia's 'arms' imports have in fact been construction costs. A. Cordesman, *Saudi Military Forces in the 1990s: The Strategic Challenge of Continued Modernization,* paper prepared for the Woodrow Wilson Center, Washington DC, 18 August 1993, p. 13.

6. In early 1996 Saudi Arabia announced the construction of a new military city and port at Jizan. J. Bruce, 'Saudis Building Military City on Yemen Border,' *JDW*, 15 May 1996, p. 3.
7. This section draws on my article: 'Saudi Arabia's Military Build-up—An Extravagant Error?' *JIR*, November 1994, pp. 500-505.
8. J. Bruce, 'Build-up to continue despite revenue drop,' *JDW*, 10 July 1996, pp. 30-33.
9. Cordesman, *Saudi Military Forces in the 1990s: The Strategic Challenge of Continued Modernization*, p. 18.
10. *Ibid.*
11. T. Dahy, *The Military Organization as an Agent for Modernization in the Third World: Case Study —National Guard in Saudi Arabia* (PhD Thesis, University of Florida, 1988), pp. 89-98.
12. Lt. Col. D.P. Hughes, 'Battle for Khafji: 29 Jan/1 Feb 1991,' *Army Quarterly & Defence Journal*, January 1994, pp. 13-22; Cordesman, *Saudi Military Forces in the 1990s: The Strategic Challenge of Continued Modernization*, pp. 28-9.
13. 'Expanding Saudi's Elite Fighting Force,' *JDW*, 24 January 1996, p. 17-18.
14. Half in store.
15. Cordesman, *Saudi Military Forces in the 1990s*, p. 22; 'Trials for Giat's Leclerc in Saudi Contract Bid,' *JDW*, 5 August 1995, p. 16; 'Desert Challenger Sets Out to Win Saudi Deal,' *JDW*, 17 January 1996, p. 15.
16. If Leclercs or Challengers are purchased instead this will make little difference to the balance. Their capabilities are similar to the M1A2 but logistical and integration problems associated with fielding different MBT types will reduce their effectiveness.
17. Estimate based on total order.
18. Estimate since some sources say the Commandoes are being replaced by the LAVs.
19. Cordesman, *Saudi Military Forces in the 1990s: The Strategic Challenge of Continued Modernization*, p. 24.
20. 'LAV-AG Decision Still Expected from SANG,' *Jane's Defence Contracts*, May 1996, p. 5.
21. It is assumed that older towed artillery and mortars will be phased out by 2005.
22. See footnote 21.
23. Cordesman, *Saudi Military Forces in the 1990s: The Strategic Challenge of Continued Modernization*, p. 25.
24. *Ibid.*

25. 'Build-up to Continue Despite Revenue Drop,' *JDW*.
26. J. Nadel, 'Logistics Lesson,' in B. Watson, ed., *Military Lessons of the Gulf War* (London, Greenhill Books, 1993), pp. 167-173; Lt Gen. W.G. Pagonis with J. Cruikshank, *Moving Mountains: Lessons in Leadership and Logistics from the Gulf War* (Boston, MA, Harvard Business School Press, 1992).
27. A former Western defence attaché pointed out that the Saudis have had great difficulty retaining their trained maintenance personnel as many tend to leave the service to go into business within 2-3 years after the completion of their training. As a result, much of the older equipment, such as M-60s, is routinely non-operational. Private information from a former Western defence attaché to Riyadh, May 1996.
28. 'Hughes Beats Saudi Deadline,' *JDW*, 11 November 1995, p. 11.
29. B. Starr, 'USA, Saudi Arabia Plan 'Crisis' Co-operation,' *JDW*, 13 November 1992, p. 16.
30. Cordesman, *Saudi Military Forces in the 1990s: The Strategic Challenge of Continued Modernization*, p. 48.
31. Cordesman, *op. cit.* pp. 44-5.
32. N. Cook, 'GCC Air Forces,' *JDW*, 24 April 1996, pp. 18-23.
33. 'Saudi MCMV,' *JDW*, 9 December 1995, p. 13.
34. Cordesman, *op.cit.* p. 31-35; Jane's *Sentinel*.

CHAPTER 4
OTHER GCC STATES

The remaining five GCC states—Bahrain, Kuwait, Qatar, the United Arab Emirates and Oman—are all engaged in military expansion programmes. Bahrain is limited by its economic problems and is dependent on US and Saudi assistance. Kuwait has ambitious plans to rebuild its armed forces but the programme is being slowed by fiscal constraints. Qatar is starting from a low base but is investing heavily. The UAE, led by Abu Dhabi, is in the midst of a costly and far reaching expansion effort. Oman's choices are seriously limited by the need to cope with its budgetary problems. Nonetheless, overall the smaller GCC states are substantially reshaping and upgrading their armed forces. They will become much more powerful over the next decade.

Bahrain

Bahrain is heavily dependent on Saudi Arabia for finance and protection, both from external and from internal threats. At the same time, it is further developing its defence ties with the US. It is therefore unlikely to act on its own in a military sense, except perhaps for minor skirmishing with Qatar. At the same time, the regime's close ties to Saudi Arabia make Bahrain the GCC state the most likely to cooperate militarily with the Kingdom.[1]

Manama sees Iran, not Iraq as the main threat, especially in light of a long tradition of Iranian subversion of Bahrain's *Shi'ite* population.[2] By itself, though, it is unlikely to be able to repel a determined Iranian air and naval assault. It is also concerned at its territorial dispute with Qatar and is building up forces on the disputed Hawar islands. Although the Bahraini Air Force and Navy currently outmatch their Qatari equivalents, Qatar's ambitious procurement programme could redress this balance over the next five to ten years.

Other GCC States

The Bahrain Defence Force (BDF) has one armoured brigade, with two tank battalions and a reconnaissance battalion; an infantry brigade with two mechanised and one motorised battalions and an artillery brigade with four gun batteries and a MRL battery.

Bahrain's modernisation programme has been helped by the willingness of NATO states to cascade surplus equipment to the emirate. The army's 13 M110A2 203mm SP howitzers were cascaded from the Dutch armed forces. Further modernisation programmes include the supply of 60 surplus M60A3s with upgraded engines by the US. The deal was agreed in January 1995 and this study assumes that the tanks will be in service by the year 2000. In addition, the Netherlands is providing 25 surplus YPR-765 AIFVs. It is assumed that these will be in service by the year 2000. No further major acquisitions are planned.

MBT

Type	Role	1995	2000	2005
M-60A3	MBT	106-120	166-180	166-180
Total	**MBT**	**106-120**	**166-180**	**166-180**

ARV/AIFV/APC

Type	Role	1995	2000	2005
AML-90	ARV	22	22	22
Saladin	ARV	8	8	-3
Ferret	ARV	8-10	8-10	-4
Shorland	ARV	8-10	8-10	8-10
Total	**ARV**	**56-60**	**56-60**	**30-32**
YPR-765	AIFV	-	25	25
Total	**AIFV**	**-**	**25**	**25**

AT-105 Saxon	APC	10	10	10
Panhard M-3	APC	110	110	110
M-113A2	APC	115	115	115
Total	**APC**	**235**	**235**	**235**

Artillery

Type	Role	1995	2000	2005
203mm M-110	SP How	13	13	13
Total	**SP Artillery**	**13**	**13**	**13**
155mm M-198	How (towed)	28	28	28
105mm lt. gun	How (towed)	8	8	8
Total	**Towed Artillery**	**36**	**36**	**36**
MLRS 227mm	MRL	9	9	9
Total	**MRL**	**9**	**9**	**9**
120mm	Mortar	9	9	9
81mm	Mortar	9	9	9
Total	**Mortar**	**18**	**18**	**18**

Anti-Tank Weapons

Type	Role	1995	2000	2005
120mm MOBAT	RCL	6	6	6
106mm M-40A1	RCL	30	30	30
Total	**RCL**	**36**	**36**	**36**
BGM-71A TOW	ATGW	15-60	15-60	15-60
Total	**ATGW**	**15-60**	**15-60**	**15-60**

The air force has a squadron of 12 F-16C/D fighters and a squadron of 12 F-5E/F FGAs. Negotiations are underway with the US regarding the swapping of the F-5s for 18 US Navy F-16Ns, which would be upgraded. The other option is the purchase of ex-US Air Force

Other GCC States

F-16A/Bs. This study assumes that 18 F-16s of some description will be purchased in the near future but that they will not be in service until the year 2005. The F-5s are meanwhile phased out.[5]

Combat Aircraft

Type	Role	1995	2000	2005
F-16C/D	Fighter	12	12	12
Total	**Fighter**	**12**	**12**	**12**
F-5E/F	FGA	12	12	-
F-16A/B or N	FGA	-	-	18
Total	**FGA**	**12**	**12**	**18**
Total combat air		**24**	**24**	**30**

The air force has 8-10 AB212 armed utility helicopters but has been discussing the purchase of up to a dozen AH-64A Apaches from the US. In 1995 a contract was signed with Hughes for 16 further AH-1E Cobra gunships, to supplement 14 ordered in 1994.[6] This indicates that Bahrain is postponing a decision on the Apaches. This study assumes that the 30 Cobras will be in service by the year 2000. By 2005, 12 Apaches are assumed to be in service, replacing the AB-212s.

Helicopters
(Armed only)

Type	Role	1995	2000	2005
AB-212	Attack Helo	8-10	8-10	-
AH-1 Cobra	Attack Helo	-	30	30
AH-64 Apache	Attack Helo	-	-	12
Total	**Attack Helo**	**8-10**	**38-40**	**42**

Bahrain's small navy has been developed for coastal protection. One of its major roles appears to be to support army positions on the

The Changing Military Balance in the Gulf

disputed Hawar islands. At the end of 1995 it received the ex-US Navy Oliver Hazard Perry class frigate.

Naval Vessels

Type	1995	2000	2005
Frigate	-	1	1
Corvette	2	2	2
Missile Craft	4	4	4
Fast Attack Craft	4	4	4

Kuwait

Although it has sought to build up its military since liberation, the emirate knows that it must rely on outside powers for its protection from Iraq. Kuwait could now certainly put up a better show than in 1990, assuming the government reacted in time and deployed its forces, but sheer weight of numbers would still tell. Therefore, much of Kuwait's arms acquisition effort has been directed by the need to secure its alliances with the five permanent members of the UN Security Council.[7]

The Kuwaiti armed forces are nonetheless becoming a more credible and effective force. The proposals of an Anglo-American Defence Review Group which laid out plans for the revamped armed forces were only formally accepted in 1995 by the Minister of Defence but arms purchases since liberation have been proceeding informally in line with the recommendations of this review.

The overall security strategy envisages a three-tiered approach. First, Kuwait will seek to build up forces able to act as a front-line 'tripwire' in case of future Iraqi attacks. Second, Kuwait will strengthen its strategic and military ties with allies through joint exercises and

Other GCC States

training. Third, the military link with the US armed forces will be bolstered to enable US forces to reinforce the Emirate rapidly in a crisis.

The armed forces' operational plan in case of an invasion would be to secure key locations for reinforcing US troops, channel invading forces into selected corridors where they can be delayed and where armoured formations can be broken up.[8] In order to implement this plan Kuwait is expanding and reorganising its armed forces. The reforms are being aided by some 30 British and 80 US military advisers.

Kuwait faces two crucial problems which are hampering the expansion of its armed forces —financial constraints and manpower shortages. Kuwait's acquisition plans are laid out in the framework of a 12 year KD3.5bn ($11.715bn) plan to run from 1992 to 2004.[9]

The draft 1995/96 budget had proposed a cut of eight per cent in total defence spending to (KD849m) $2.88bn. The cuts were to come from the supplementary account for arms purchases, to fall from $1.7bn to $1.38bn. Other defence expenditure was to grow from $1.44bn to $1.54bn. This cut was queried by some analysts who noted that Kuwait had already agreed to a $529m deal to buy eight patrol boats from France while negotiations with McDonnell Douglas to buy 16 AH64 Apaches worth $500-$692m were well advanced.[10] Nonetheless, the government appears determined to curb its procurement spending, meaning that purchases are likely to be stretched out.[11] In addition, Kuwait has tended to opt for cheaper Russian equipment.[12]

Kuwait's second problem is more fundamental—its limited population. In order to man the proposed armed forces, Kuwait needs 5000 officers and 40 000 other ranks. The target for officers has almost been reached but there are only some 20 000 other ranks serving. Some 60 per cent of the armed forces personnel are *bidoun*,

55

a group which the government is trying to ease out, making the manning problem even worse. It is highly unlikely that the required numbers can be recruited from Kuwait's remaining native population.

The recruitment problem is worst in the army, which offers few chances for foreign travel or training but does require hard slog in the desert. It is also acute in certain specific areas. For instance, in order to keep its 40 F/A-18s operational, the Air Force will have to train 100 pilots. In view of the highly specialised skills demanded of fighter pilots, the high costs and length of training, it is unlikely that this requirement will be fulfilled. Without recourse to the enlistment of foreigners, it is probable that Kuwait's forces will remain undermanned.

Another manifestation of the manpower problem is the fact that, for the foreseeable future, the Kuwaiti armed forces will continue to rely on civilian contractors to provide even first line maintenance for their equipment. Contractors deployed to the field with the army in October 1994, but it must be in doubt whether they would be willing to stay at their posts in a shooting war. The Ministry of Defence says that it would like to build up an indigenous maintenance capability but this is not even on the drawing board. [13]

Even if financial and manpower problems are overcome, the delivery and absorption of the new hardware will take time. The full complement of MBTs and AIFVs will not arrive until 1997 and it will take some years before the army, air force and air defence forces learn how to use their hardware.[14] It is unlikely to be earlier than the turn of the century before command and control systems are integrated and operational doctrines are fully formulated, understood and absorbed.[15]

Nonetheless, the military's Western advisers are keen to praise the advances that are being made in the most important part of any military—the human 'software.' The air defence forces, which are now operating their new Shorts Starburst short range air defence missile, come in for particular praise. In March 1996 the British Army opened a Command and Staff College in the emirate in which Kuwaiti instructors will work with their British counterparts. This is seen as a significant recognition on the part of the Kuwaitis of the vital importance of planning and staff work in a modern army.

Ground Forces

Kuwait plans to field an army with two mechanised brigades equipped with American Abrams M1 MBT and British Desert Warrior AIFVs and one mechanised brigade equipped with Yugoslav M-84 MBTs and Russian BMP-3 AIFVs. A fourth, reserve, brigade is also planned to be equipped with any hardware that remains such as American M-113 APCs. These brigades will be highly trained, with considerable help from the US and UK, and taught to operate as mobile, combined arms entities. They will be supported by artillery systems including the Russian *Smerch* mobile multiple rocket launchers and upgraded 155mm guns.[16]

MBT

Type	Role	1995	2000	2005
Abrams M1-A2	MBT	50	218	218
M-84	MBT	150-200	150-200	150-200
Chieftain	MBT	20 (in store)	-	-
Total	**MBT**	**220-270**	**368-418**	**368-418**

The army has ordered 218 Abrams M1-A2 MBTs, along with 46 M-88 Armoured Recovery Vehicles. These will be in service by the end of the decade.[17] Kuwait is reportedly seeking to upgrade its M-84s to T-72M standard.[18] The Army's Chieftains, including 48 that were returned by Iraq in a poor condition, along with a number of Vickers Mk1s, have been placed in store prior to being scrapped. It is assumed they will be out of the inventory by the end of the decade.

ARV/AIFV/APC

Type	Role	1995	2000	2005
Scorpion	ARV	10 (in store)	-	-
Piranha	ARV	-	88	88
Total	**ARV**	**10** (in store)	**88**	**88**
BMP-2	AIFV	46	46	46
BMP-3	AIFV	76	136	136
Desert Warrior	AIFV	8	254	254
Total	**AIFV**	**130**	**436**	**436**
M-113	APC	153	278	278
Fahd	APC	40-44	40-44	40-44
M-577	APC	6	6	6
Total	**APC**	**199-203**	**324-328**	**324-328**

In order to build its planned mechanised units, the army has ordered a further 125 M-113 APCs, 88 Piranha wheeled ARVs, 60 BMP-3 AIFVs and a total of 254 GKN Warrior AIFVs.[19] It is assumed that these will be in service by the end of the decade but that the Scorpions will meanwhile be phased out.

Artillery

Type	Role	1995	2000	2005
155mm M-109A2	SP How	22	22	22
155mm GCT	SP How	18 (in store)	18	18
155mm F-3	SP How	16	16	16
Total	**SP Artillery**	**38** (+18 in store)	**56**	**56**
300mm *Smerch*	MRL	-	27	27
Total	**MRL**	**-**	**27**	**27**

120mm	Mortar	(12)[20]	(12)	(12)
107mm M-30	SP Mortar	6	6	6
81mm	SP Mortar	6	6	6
81mm	Mortar	45	45	45
Total	**Mortar**	**57 (69)**	**57 (69)**	**57 (69)**

Kuwait ordered 27 *Smerch* MRLs from Russia in 1994, choosing them over the US MLRS on grounds of price and its superior range to the American system.[21] It is assumed that these will be in service by 2000 and that the 155mm GCT howitzers will be brought into service.[22]

Anti-Tank Weapons

Type	Role	1995	2000	2005
84mm Carl Gustav	RCL	200	200	200
Total	**RCL**	**200**	**200**	**200**
M-901 SP TOW	ATGW	8	8	8
HMMWV TOW	ATGW	60	60	60
Total	**ATGW**	**68**	**68**	**68**

Air Force

The Air Force is seen as the key support arm both to protect Kuwaiti air space and to provide close air support to the army. Its main assets are 40 American F/A-18 Hornet multi-role fighters organised into two squadrons, the 9th and the 25th. In addition, the Kuwaiti Air Force still has 8-15 Mirage F-1 fighters in no 18 and no 61 squadrons based at Ahmad al-Jabir airbase. These may be phased out in the period under review.

Combat Aircraft

Type	Role	1995	2000	2005
Mirage F-1	Fighter	8-15	8-15	-
Total	Fighter	8-15	8-15	-
F/A-18	FGA	40	40	40
Hawk	Strike	12	12	12
Strikemaster	Strike	8	-23	-
Total	FGA/strike	60	52	52
Total combat air		68-75	60-67	52

Battlefield support is at present provided by Gazelle light helicopters armed with HOT ATGW. These will be reinforced with the deployment of 16 AH-64 Apache attack helicopters along with 500 Hellfire ATGWs which have been ordered. Negotiations are continuing for the purchase of up to eight more Apaches.[24] This study assumes that 16 Apaches are in service by the year 2000 and a further eight by 2005.

Helicopters
(Armed only)

Type	Role	1995	2000	2005
SA-342 Gazelle	Attack Helo	16	16	16
AH-64 Apache	Attack Helo	-	16	24
Total	Attack Helo	16	32	40

Navy

Kuwait's small navy was put out of action during the Gulf War and is only now being rebuilt. Its main bases at Ras al-Jalaya and Umm Qasr are being rebuilt. It now has only two Exocet-armed missile craft, as well as between two and four large patrol boats. In 1995 it signed a $500 million contract with DCN-International of France to purchase eight P37BRL patrol boats. The 42 metre ships will be delivered by 1999 and will be equipped with anti-ship and anti-aircraft missiles.[25]

Naval Vessels

Type	1995	2000	2005
Missile Craft	2	2	2
Patrol boats	2-4	10-12	10-12

Qatar

In recent years Qatar, under the influence of Sheikh Hamad bin Khalifah Al Thani, who became emir in 1995, has pursued an independent foreign policy often at odds with its GCC neighbours. Unsure of its own identity as a nation state and afraid of Saudi domination, Qatar has attempted to balance off larger powers by maintaining good ties with Iran and Iraq at the same time as drawing closer to the US and Israel. [26]

Although a member of the GCC, Qatar feels that it has little to fear from Iran or Iraq. Its main concern is Saudi Arabia which has long looked down on the Al Thani and questioned the right of Qatar to call itself a sovereign state.[27] Although Qatari officials will not admit it publicly, the main threat is Saudi Arabia and the armed forces often exercise against this threat in the south of the country.[28] Qatar is also concerned about its territorial dispute with Bahrain. Qatar claims that it should be given control of the Hawar islands and has submitted its case to the International Court of Justice. Doha feels that, since Bahrain is a close ally of Saudi Arabia, Bahraini policy towards the islands dispute is part of the Saudi strategic threat.[29] Although there is no sign that Qatar wishes to militarise the dispute, as it did by provoking a clash in 1986, it is concerned that the Bahraini Defence Force has positioned tanks and missiles on the islands, within artillery range of Qatar's Dukhan oil field. Qatar has not similarly fortified its coastline.

Qatar's armed forces are the smallest and weakest of all the GCC states and against any potential opponent could do no more than put up a token fight. Nonetheless, they are upgrading their equipment and, in certain areas, have a good reputation.

A large proportion of the rank and file are Omanis and Yemenis, regarded as tough fighters by military observers. Many of the officers are highly competent Jordanians while Qatari officers have a fair reputation. The Air Force in particular is lauded by its foreign allies. It is inspected annually by a British Royal Air Force (RAF) team and reaches the same standards of individual training as the RAF. The army, however, despite its respectable performance at Khafji during the Second Gulf War, scores poorly in exercises with US and French forces. The armed forces lack planning and command and staff ability.[30]

Qatar's arms purchasing policy is, like that of its neighbours, driven as much by questions of prestige as of operational effectiveness. Its small air force has ordered a dozen Mirage 2000-5 fighters. Although these advanced French jets complement the Mirage F-1s in service, they are far too sophisticated for Qatar's 900 man air force to operate effectively.

Although it maintains very close military ties with France, the key to Qatar's security strategy is its alliance with the US. Doha has sought to win American favour by pursuing normalisation of relations with Israel and by allowing US participation in the development of its North Field gas project. In military terms, the Qataris have allowed the US to construct a site for the pre-positioning of up to a brigade's worth of armour and mechanised fighting vehicles. The site, near Dukhan, will be ready by January 1997 and will involve the stationing of a small number of US servicemen to guard and maintain the equipment. The Qataris are however being careful not to allow the

Other GCC States

American giant to trample on them. Although the US Marines want to preposition a brigade's worth of hardware, the Qataris envisage the presence of only a regiment of 34 tanks.[31]

In terms of ground forces, the key development underway is the replacement of Qatar's aging AMX-30 tanks. Britain's Vickers is offering the Challenger and France's Giat the Leclerc while the US hopes to sell Abrams M1. Abu Dhabi bought the Leclerc and France has been remarkably successful at marketing itself in Qatar in recent years. Whichever tank is chosen, 50 units are likely to be purchased and will equip the army's one armoured battalion.

Qatar's four mechanised infantry battalions are now equipped with AMX-10P AIFVs and VAB APCs. Small numbers of assorted APCs are being acquired but no requirement has yet been issued for a new generation of AIFVs.

MBT

Type	Role	1995	2000	2005
AMX-30	MBT	24	-	-
Challenger/ Leclerc/M1/	MBT	-	50	50
Total	**MBT**	**24**	**50**	**50**

ARV/AIFV/APC

Type	Role	1995	2000	2005
VBL	ARV	6	6	6
AMX-10RC	ARV	12	12	12
V-150	ARV	8	8	8
Saracen	ARV	6	-	-
Total	**ARV**	**32**	**26**	**26**
AMX-10P	AIFV	40	40	40
Total	**AIFV**	**40**	**40**	**40**

VAB	APC	160	160	160
AMX-VCI	APC	12	12	12
Fahd	APC	-	10	10
Total	**APC**	**172**	**182**	**182**

Artillery

Type	Role	1995	2000	2005
155mm AMX Mk F-3	SP How	28	28	28
Total	**SP Artillery**	**28**	**28**	**28**
155mm G5	How (towed)	12	12	12
Total	**Towed Artillery**	**12**	**12**	**12**
ASTROS II	MRL	4	4	4
Total	**MRL**	**4**	**4**	**4**
120mm	Mortar	15	15	15
81mm L16	Mortar	20	20	20
81mm L16	SP Mortar	4	4	4
Total	**Mortar**	**39**	**39**	**39**

Anti-Tank Weapons

Type	Role	1995	2000	2005
84mm Carl Gustav	RCL	?	?	?
Total	**RCL**	**?**	**?**	**?**
Milan	ATGW	100	100	100
HOT	ATGW	20	20	20
HOT/VAB SP	ATGW	24	24	24
Total	**ATGW**	**144**	**144**	**144**

Qatar's Mirage F-1s are being sold to Spain and deliveries of 12 Mirage 2000-5, in the multi-role version, will begin in 1997. Qatar is also considering replacing or supplementing its Alpha jet trainers with Hawks.[32]

Combat Aircraft

Type	Role	1995	2000	2005
Mirage F-1	FGA	6	-	-
Mirage 2000-5	FGA	-	12	12
Alpha Jet	FGA	6	6	6
Total	FGA	12	18	18
Total combat air		12	18	18

Helicopters
(Armed only)

Type	Role	1995	2000	2005
SA-342L Gazelle	Attack Helo	12	12	12
Total	Attack Helo	12	12	12

Qatar's navy is being substantially upgrade with the purchase of four *Vita* class fast attack craft from Vosper Thorneycroft. The first two were accepted in June 1996 and the others will be delivered in late 1997. These 56m ships, armed with Exocets and Sadral SAMs will replace the six *Barzan*-class patrol craft. In addition, Qatar's *Damsah* class (Combatante III) fast attack craft will be upgraded and refurbished.

Naval Vessels

Type	1995	2000	2005
Missile Craft	3	7	7
Patrol boats	6	-	-

United Arab Emirates

The United Arab Emirates (UAE) federal armed forces were created on 5 May 1976 by the merger of the Trucial Oman Scouts and the Abu Dhabi Defence Forces. They are now divided into the Western

Command (Abu Dhabi with some 75 per cent of the total force), Central Command (Dubai), and Northern Command (Ras al-Khaimah). This unified force, however, exists only on paper. Even the smaller emirates jealously guard their military independence. For instance, Sharjah's tiny Emiri guard has its own Military Institute in parallel to the Federal Military Training School in Al Ain.[33]

The important division is between Dubai and Abu Dhabi.[34] Dubai has always tried to remain separate with its own two brigades and air wing while Ras al-Khaimah and Sharjah look to past glories with their own 'brigades'. Dubai has also sought to maintain its own arms procurement channels (and so retains strong links to the UK whereas Abu Dhabi is closer to France). The Abu Dhabi armed forces nonetheless dominate the UAE military.[35] Abu Dhabi's financial dominance has meant that the others are losing their significance. It ordered 390 Leclerc MBTs and 46 armoured recovery vehicles in 1993 and is in the market for up to 80 advanced combat aircraft as well as stand off missiles.

Complicating defence planning is the fact that the different emirates in the UAE have different threat perceptions. Dubai and Sharjah do not see Iran as a threat but Abu Dhabi, through the General Headquarters (GHQ) dominates strategic thinking and is concerned at Iran's military buildup and aggressive statements concerning Abu Musa and the Tunbs.[36] GHQ's ambitious air and naval expansion plans are intended to give the UAE the ability to protect the UAE's offshore oil platforms and maritime trade routes from Iranian naval and air interference. It also aims to be able to defend its airspace against Iranian air attacks and to threaten retaliation for Iranian SSM attacks. The motive for the massive upgrade of Abu Dhabi's ground forces is less clear in view of Iran's limited amphibious lift capabilities. These plans may be explained by the fact that there are still latent tensions between the UAE, Oman and Saudi Arabia over their mutual border, especially with regard to the Buraimi oasis.[37]

Ground Forces

The UAE ground forces currently have six brigades. Two brigades (al-Dhafra and Khalid bin Walid) are under the direct control of GHQ. The Badr brigade is a poorly equipped, motorised infantry force raised by Ras al-Khaimah. The Yarmouk brigade is likewise a light infantry force, though equipped with Scorpions, raised by Sharjah. Dubai's two brigades are more heavily equipped and are being upgraded. Dubai is now equipping its brigades with integral air defence and artillery units. In the medium term it is likely to upgrade its forces further with the purchase of an MBT such as the T-80.

The most important development in the UAE ground forces is the modernisation programme planned by Chief of Staff Lt. General Muhammad bin Zayed Al Nahyan. He envisages cutting the size of the armed forces, in particular removing many of the 30 per cent of personnel who are expatriates, and building a smaller, mobile and more sophisticated force. Recognising that Dubai's brigades will not be under the control of GHQ for some time to come, the Chief of Staff plans to upgrade his two brigades into two armoured and two mechanised brigades by the end of the decade. The armoured brigades would each have two armoured battalions equipped with Leclerc and a mechanised battalion with BMP-3s. The mechanised brigades would have two mechanised battalions and an armoured battalion.[38]

These ambitious plans are likely to take longer than expected to fulfill, especially since Abu Dhabi has fallen into the trap of purchasing large quantities of front line hardware rather than building a balanced force. In particular, its proposed brigades lack integral air defence capabilities and are short of engineering and transport equipment to ensure long distance and off-road mobility.[39]

The Changing Military Balance in the Gulf

This study assumes that the Leclercs come into service gradually over the next decade and that the AMX-30s are concurrently phased out. In addition, it is assumed that Dubai purchases a brigade of T-80s by 2005.[40]

MBT

Type	Role	1995	2000	2005
AMX-30	MBT	95	36	-
OF-40 Mk2	MBT	36	36	36
Leclerc	MBT	2	250	390
T-80	MBT	-	-	36
Total	**MBT**	**133**	**322**	**462**

ARV/AIFV/APC

Type	Role	1995	2000	2005
Scorpion	ARV	76	76	76
AML-60/90	ARV	90-120	90-120	90-120
Saladin	ARV	50 (in store)	-	-
Ferret	ARV	20 (in store)	-	-
Total	**ARV**	**166-196 (+70in store)**	**166-196**	**166-196**
AMX-10P	AIFV	15-18	15-18	15-18
BMP-3	AIFV	330	330	330
Total	**AIFV**	**345-348**	**345-348**	**345-348**
VCR	APC	80	80	80
Panhard M-3	APC	240	240	240
EE-11 Urutu	APC	60-100	60-100	60-100
Total	**APC**	**380-400**	**380-400**	**380-400**

Other GCC States

Artillery

Type	Role	1995	2000	2005
Scud-B	SSM	6[41]	6	6
Total	**SSM**	**6**	**6**	**6**
155mm Mk F-3	SP How	18-20	18-20	18-20
155mm G-6	SP How	72-78	72-78	72-78
Total	**SP Artillery**	**90-98**	**90-98**	**90-98**
130mm Type 59-1	How (towed)	20	20	20
105mm ROF lt.	How (towed)	62	62	62
105mm M-56	How (towed)	12-18	12-18	12-18
Total	**Towed Artillery**	**94-100**	**94-100**	**94-100**
122mm FIROS-25	MRL	48	48	48
Total	**MRL**	**48**	**48**	**48**
120mm Brandt	Mortar	21	21	21
81mm	Mortar	80-110	80-110	80-110
Total	**Mortar**	**101-131**	**101-131**	**101-131**

Anti-Tank Weapons

Type	Role	1995	2000	2005
106mm	RCL	30	30	30
84mm Carl Gustav	RCL	250	250	250
Total	**RCL**	**280**	**280**	**280**
Milan/Vigilant	ATGW	230	230	230
TOW	ATGW	25-54	25-54	25-54
HOT SP	ATGW	8-20	8-20	8-20
Total	**ATGW**	**263-304**	**263-304**	**263-304**

69

Air Force

Like the ground forces, the UAE Air Force is divided between Dubai and Abu Dhabi. The Dubai Air Wing, equipped with Hawk, has a limited strike capability and operates independently of the Abu Dhabi Air Force (ADAF). The ADAF has three squadrons of Mirage fighters and FGA and two squadrons of Hawk 102s. Abu Dhabi is seeking to upgrade its air defence and strike capabilities with up to 80 advanced fighter aircraft, complemented by stand off missiles.[42] It is unclear exactly how the air force will evolve over the coming decade since the UAE is considering a number of different options.[43] This study assumes that no new aircraft come into service by the end of the decade but that 50 are acquired by 2005.

Combat Aircraft

Type	Role	1995	2000	2005
Mirage 2000 EAD	Fighter	22	22	-
Total	Fighter	22	22	-
Mirage 2000E	FGA	9	9	-
Hawk 102	FGA	18	18	18
Hawk MK63A	FGA	14-16	14-16	14-16
Mirage 2000-5/MiG-29/F-15/F16/Tornado	FGA	-	-	50
Total	FGA/strike	41	41	82
Mirage 2000 RAD	Recce	8	8	-
Total combat air		71[44]	71	82

Helicopters
(Armed only)

Type	Role	1995	2000	2005
AH-64A Apache	Attack Helo	20	20	20
SA-342 Gazelle	Attack Helo	10	10	10
Total	Attack Helo	30	30	30

Navy

The UAE navy is undergoing major expansion and is seeking to make the transition to a new generation of missile-armed frigates. At present the navy and coastguard provide an adequate coastal defence force out to perhaps 50 miles but have no real capability to operate further afield.

In April 1996 the UAE agreed to take over two ex-Royal Netherlands Navy frigates of the *Kortenaer* S-class. The $350 million deal includes a complete overhaul of the vessels before delivery in 1997-8. The contract supersedes an earlier proposal to lease an ex-US Navy frigate. The agreement is an interim measure while the UAE considers its options for up to six newbuild frigates. Contractors in the UK, America, France, Germany and the Netherlands have been competing for the work. In addition, the UAE is considering the purchase of three minehunters, the replacement of its *Ardhana* class inshore patrol craft and the upgrading of its *Baniyas* class missile craft.[45]

If all of these plans go ahead then the UAE navy will become a powerful force with greatly increased ability to protect its coastline and offshore oil installations. This study assumes that current plans, and the necessary training, are completed by the year 2005.

Naval Vessels

Type	1995	2000	2005
Frigate	-	2	6
Corvette	2	2	2
Missile Craft	8	8	8
MCM	-	3	3

Oman

Oman prides itself on having developed good relations with all of its neighbours. It has settled its disputed borders with the UAE, Saudi Arabia and Yemen. It maintains close ties to Tehran, even to the extent of proposing joint naval exercises. As a result of its successful diplomatic policies, the Sultanate faces few immediate external threats.[46] Nonetheless, there is a residue of suspicion about Riyadh's hegemonistic ambitions and latent tensions with the UAE.[47] There is also the ever present possibility of being caught up in a confrontation between Iran and Oman's Western or GCC allies.

Oman's armed forces have the reputation of being the best trained in the GCC. Their extensive operational experience in the Dhofar campaign and their intimate links with the British armed forces have ensured that they maintain a fair standard of training and professionalism. They are not the best equipped and the need to conserve resources has forced them to take more modest but sustainable procurement decisions.[48] As part of the Sultanate's economic reforms instituted in the mid-1990s they have had to bear their share of fiscal cutbacks. Although projected spending on defence and security rose from RO 667 million in 1995 to RO 699 million in 1996, they are unlikely to expand or modernise significantly in the near future.[49] From 1997 onwards, the armed forces budget is to be cut, leading to further delays in procurement.[50]

Unlike its GCC neighbours, Oman has no trouble filling the ranks of its armed forces with nationals. It does however continue to rely heavily on foreign assistance in its officer corps, despite the Omanisation of its senior ranks. Britain provides up to 130 loan service officers and NCOs in addition to several hundred officers serving on contracts. There are also substantial numbers of Pakistani and Jordanian officers on loan to the armed forces.

Royal Army of Oman (RAO)

The headquarters of the 25 000 strong RAO is a divisional-level body based at Muaskar al Murtafa (MAM). The country is divided into three military zones. The 23rd Infantry Brigade is headquartered at MAM, the 11th Infantry Brigade at Salalah and the Musandam Defence Force (an independent rifle company) is based on the Musandam Peninsula.

The RAO ORBAT includes eight infantry regiments (battalions) in trucks, though one is being converted to Piranha APCs. The two armoured regiments each have two squadrons of 14 MBTs and two squadrons of 14 Scorpions. There is also an armoured reconnaissance regiment, with armoured cars, and an infantry reconnaissance regiment with three companies. There are four artillery regiments (battalions), two with field howitzers, one with medium guns and one equipped for air defence. The Sultan's parachute regiment (battalion) also comes under RAO command.

The 6500 strong Royal Guard of Oman is a brigade-strength force in charge of the Sultan's security. It has an armoured squadron and two infantry battalions equipped with VAB APCs. Two Special Forces regiments, of around 700 men each, come under the command of the Royal Guard.[51]

The main development in Oman's armoured forces is the replacement of its Chieftain Mk 7s with Challenger 2s.[52] These are being supported by the supply of nine tank transporters and four Armoured Repair and Recovery Vehicles. Oman retains an option to purchase a further 18 Challenger MBTs but financial problems have delayed this decision. In the meantime, Oman is to receive 50 M60A3 MBTs on a no-cost lease basis from the US. These should be delivered before the end of 1997.[53] Oman will subsequently phase out its remaining Chieftains and M60A1s.

MBT

Type	Role	1995	2000	2005
Challenger 2	MBT	12	18	18
M-60A3	MBT	43-47	93-97	93-97
M-60A1	MBT	6	6	-
Chieftain Mk7/15	MBT	24	12	-
Total	MBT	85-89	129-133	111-115

In 1994 Oman ordered 80 GKN MOWAG Piranha. Variants include APCs, armed with a 12.7mm machine gun, ambulances, artillery observation, command, recovery and 81mm mortar carriers. Final deliveries will be in 1997. It has an option on 46 more, including anti-tank versions, which could be delivered after 1997.[54] This study assumes that this option will not be exercised in the coming decade because of defence cutbacks but that they will be purchased by 2005. Meanwhile, the older APCs, Spartan and Sultan, will be phased out.

ARV/AIFV/APC

Type	Role	1995	2000	2005
Scorpion	ARV	37	37	37
VBC-90	ARV	6	6	6
Total	ARV	43	43	43
Piranha	AIFV	20	80	126
Total	AIFV	20	80	126
VAB	APC	14	14	14
Fahd	APC	25	25	25
Spartan	APC	6	6	-
Sultan	APC	13	13	-
Total	APC	58	58	39

Oman's artillery is being upgraded by the delivery of 24 G-6 self-propelled guns. This study assumes that older towed artillery pieces are phased out as the G-6s are brought into service.

Artillery

Type	Role	1995	2000	2005
155mm G-6	SP Gun	6	24	24
Total	**SP Artillery**	**6**	**24**	**24**
130mm Type 59-1	How (towed)	12?	-	-
130mm M-46	How (towed)	12	-	-
122mm D-30	How (towed)	30?	-	-
105mm ROF lt.	How (towed)	42	42	42
Total	**Towed Artillery**	**54-96**	**42**	**42**
120mm Brandt	Mortar	12?	12?	12?
107mm	Mortar	12-20	12-20	12-20
81mm	Mortar	54-80	54-80	54-80
Total	**Mortar**	**66-112**	**66-112**	**66-112**

Anti-Tank Weapons

Type	Role	1995	2000	2005
TOW	ATGW	18	18	18
Milan	ATGW	32-50	32-50	32-50
Total	**ATGW**	**50-68**	**50-68**	**50-68**

Royal Air Force of Oman (RAFO)

The RAFO bases its combat units at Masirah and Thumrait. Masirah is home to no 1 squadron (Strikemaster) and no 20 squadron (Jaguar). Thumrait is home to no 8 Squadron (Jaguar). Thumrait did house no 6 squadron (Hunter) but it is assumed that this has been replaced by a Hawk-equipped squadron.[55]

The RAFO has trained and operated closely with the RAF and is considered competent and well prepared. Budgetary cutbacks have, however, recently forced it to curtail its training. The RAFO is moderately well equipped with munitions, including AIM-9P Sidewinder AAMs and Exocet AM-39 anti-ship missiles.

Combat Aircraft

Type	Role	1995	2000	2005
Jaguar	FGA	19[56]	19	19
Hawk	FGA/recce	12	12	12
BAC-167 Strikemaster	close sprt	11	11	-
Total combat air		42	42	31

The Air Force is replacing its 15 Hawker Hunters with 12 BAe Hawk 200 fighters and four Hawk 100 advanced trainers. It is considering F-16A/Bs or Mirage 2000-5 to replace its Jaguars. Budget cutbacks are, however, likely to delay a decision on this requirement. This study assumes that no decision is made over the next decade. The Strikemasters are likely to be phased out of their close support role.

Royal Navy of Oman (RNO)

The RNO has a major role in protecting Oman's coastal waters and monitoring the Strait of Hormuz. It works closely with the US and British navies in carrying out these roles. It is undergoing an ambitious modernisation and expansion programme. Two 83m missile corvettes are being built by Vosper Thorneycroft and will be equipped with Active Towed Array Sonar. In addition, three P-400 fast attack craft have been ordered from France. Oman would like to purchase another five of these vessels.[57] Oman also has two LSTs.

Naval Vessels

Type	1995	2000	2005
Corvette	-	2	2
Missile Craft	4	4	4
Fast Attack Craft	4	7	12
Amphibious	2	2	2

Notes

1. On the history of the Bahraini armed forces, see: H. Bin Isa Al Khalifa, *First Light: Modern Bahrain and its Heritage* (London, Kegan Paul International, 1994).
2. 'Bahrain foils pro-Iran plot to overthrow government,' *Guardian*, 4 June 1996.
3. Assuming that the Saladins are phased out by 2005.
4. Assuming that the Ferrets are phased out by 2005.
5. P. Finnegan, 'Bahrain Puts Air Defense at Top of Upgrade List,' *Defense News*, 10-16 June, 1996, p. 16.
6. 'Seeking low cost modernization,' *JDW*, 30 September 1995, pp. 32-33.
7. A.K. Pasha, 'Kuwait's Quest for Security,' *India Quarterly*, October 1993, pp. 1-16; 'Dependence on US leaves Kuwait few choices,' *Financial Times*, 28 October 1994; J. De Lestapis, 'Striking a strategic security balance,' *JDW*, 29 July 1995, pp. 23-24. On the background to Kuwait's foreign policy, see: A. Abdul-Reda Asiri, *Kuwait's Foreign Policy: City State in World Politics* (Boulder, CO, Westview, 1990).
8. 'Three-tier plan aims at stronger Kuwait,' *JDW*, 20 February 1993.
9. 'Kuwaiti rearmament Feels Budget Squeeze,' *Middle East Reporter*, 25 February 1995, p. 16.
10. 'Cash Crunch May Stall Kuwaiti Arms,' *Defense News*, 28 November -4 December 1994, p. 1 & 36.
11. J. Bruce, 'Kuwait cuts back on its high military spending,' *JDW*, 27 May 1995, p. 5. The draft 1996/7 budget planned a 20 per cent cut in the arms procurement account. 'Finance minister planning to reduce arms budget by 20 per cent,' *Al-Sharq al-Awsat*, 8 May 1996, in SWB/ME, 10 May 1996, p. 8.
12. Three BMP-3s can be purchased for the price of one Warrior.
13. Before the invasion, Kuwait's 18 British MBTs were kept running by a British REME team since the Kuwaitis proved unwilling to do the routine maintenance necessary for field operations. Interview.
14. For surveys of Kuwait's acquisition plans, see: 'Market Briefing: Kuwait,' *JDW*, 29 July 1995, pp. 17-35; C. Foss, 'Bidding for the Main Chance,' *JDW*, 15 January 1994.
15. 'Kuwaiti army puts on an unconvincing display,' *Financial Times*, 11 October 1994.
16. 'Three-tier plan aims at stronger Kuwait,' *JDW*, 20 February 1993; J. De Lastapis, 'Low dollar gives USA edge over rivals,' *JDW*, 29 July 1995, pp. 26-32.
17. 'Tanks roll in,' *Times*, 1 December 1994.

18. Beaver, ed, 'Kuwait,' *Jane's Sentinel Regional Security Assessment*, p. 11.
19. 'Bidding for the main chance,' *JDW*, 15 January 1994, p. 20-21.
20. Returned by Iraq in a poor condition. It is not clear whether these will be refurbished and put back into service.
21. C. Foss, 'Multiple rocket duel over Kuwaiti order,' *JDW*, 16 April 1993; C. Foss, 'Kuwait's money buys more than artillery firepower,' *JDW*, 20 August 1994, p. 21.
22. Further artillery purchases are likely. P. Finnegan, 'Kuwait Shifts Focus From Politics to Weapon Quality,' *Defense News*, 10-16 June 1996, p. 8.
23. Assumes Strikemasters are phased out.
24. 'More Apaches Wanted,' *JDW*, 22 October 1994. Kuwait may purchase Black Hawks instead of Apaches.
25. J. Bruce, 'Kuwait signs $500m patrol boat contract,' *JDW*, 8 April 1995; 'UK Companies Win Kuwait Naval Contracts,' Bankside Consultants press release 27 March 1995.
26. 'Qatar Defines Itself,' *Gulf States Newsletter*, 4 December 1995, pp. 8-11; 'Qatar Coup Could Bring Shake-Up of Gulf Politics,' *IHT*, 28 June 1995.
27. R. Said Zahlan, *The Creation of Qatar* (London, Croom Helm, 1979), pp. 80-91; L. Graz, *The Turbulent Gulf* (London, I.B. Tauris, 1992), pp. 157-167.
28. Interviews.
29. A. Jalkh, 'Le Qatar rebelle et vulnérable,' *Arabies*, April 1995, pp. 26-32.
30. Interviews.
31. 'USA moves armoured brigade into Qatar,' *JDW*, 17 January 1996; 'US Gulf Military Strategy,' *Reuter*, 20 March 1996; Interviews.
32. 'Qatar shops around,' *JDW*, 30 September 1995, pp. 37-38.
33. 'UAE: Towards a Military Confederation of the Emirates,' *APS Diplomat*, 24 March 1986.
34. For background to the internal divisions in the UAE, see: R. Said Zahlan, *The Origins of the United Arab Emirates* (London, Macmillan, 1978), pp. 196-198; A.O. Taryam, *The Establishment of the United Arab Emirates* (London, Croom Helm, 1987), pp. 197-253.
35. 'United Arab Emirates: A Federation with Unified Armed Forces,' *APS Diplomat*, 8 January 1990.
36. W.A. Rugh, 'The Foreign Policy of the United Arab Emirates,' *Middle East Journal*, Vol. 50, No. 1 (Winter 1996), pp. 57-70. For an account of divisions within the UAE's foreign policy making structure, see: H.H. al-Alkim, *The Foreign Policy of the United Arab Emirates* (London, Saqi Books, 1989).

37. Such fears are not publicly expressed. It is interesting to note, though, that many official Saudi maps portray the Kingdom's border extending deep into the Abu Dhabi emirate, not to mention into Oman and Yemen. See for instance the map in the Saudi Ministry of Planning's *Fifth Development Plan, 1990-1995.*
38. Regional Briefing: UAE,' *JDW*, 18 March 1995, pp. 38-66; Interviews.
39. Interviews.
40. F. Tusa, ' Cold comfort in desert land sales,' *MEED*, 17 March 1995, pp. 12-13.
41. Dubai.
42. 'UAE buy raises basing doubts,' *JDW*, 25 November 1995, p. 19; 'Hakim PGMs on target in first Abu Dhabi tests,' *JDW*, 9 December 1995, p. 13.
43. Options include the Mirage 2000-5 with Rafale follow on, the MiG-29M, F-16 or F-15, Tornado with European Fighter Aircraft follow on. Contenders for the stand off missile include GEC-Marconi's *Hakim* and BAe/Matra's *Apache* and variants. D. Isby, 'The Emir's New Swords,' *Military Technology*, March 1995, pp. 10-16.
44. Jane's and JCSS list 18-23 Mirage 5s in the inventory but IISS omits these. It is assumed that they are out of service.
45. J. Janssen Lok, 'UAE Navy to take over ex-Dutch Kortenaers,' *JDW*, 17 April 1996; 'Regional Briefing: UAE,' *JDW*, 18 March 1995, p. 42.
46. J. Kechichian, *Oman and the World* (Santa Monica, CA, RAND, 1995).
47. See footnote 5, above.
48. 'Oman's armed forces keep up the standard,' *JDW*, 30 September 1995, pp. 34-36.
49. Special Report 'Oman', *MEED*, 3 May 1996, pp. 9-16.
50. Interviews.
51. IISS, *The Military Balance* and Jane's *Sentinel*, interviews.
52. 'Oman signs contract for Challenger 2s,' *JDW,* 3 July 1993; 'Omani armoured might goes on parade,' *JDW*, 25 November 1995, p. 23.
53. P. Finnegan, 'Cash-Strapped Oman Weighs Upgrade to Air, Armor Forces,' *Defense News*, 10-16 June 1996, p. 12.
54. 'Oman orders 80 LAV from Piranha family,' *JDW*, 28 May 1994, p. 11.
55. IISS, *The Military Balance* and Jane's *Sentinel*, interviews.
56. Includes combat trainer versions.
57. 'RNO Modernisation,' *Oman Daily Observer*, 12 December 1993; 'Oman buys ATAS for its new corvettes, *JDW*, 18 September 1993.

CHAPTER 5
MEASURING THE BALANCE

Having described the force building plans of the Gulf states in previous chapters, it is time to draw some conclusions regarding the evolving military balance in the Gulf. Judging strategic balances is a notoriously inexact art and this paper makes no undue claims to precision. The aim is not to arrive at an exact measure of the present or future balance, since any such assessment would be dependent on too many unpredictable and unquantifiable variables. Instead, the aim is to highlight broad trends in the evolving strategic balance.

This chapter will first set the context by illustrating the geostrategic weights of the states comprising the Gulf regional system. In the medium term these relative weights are assumed to be immutable and so underpin the regional balance of power. Discussion will then move onto certain measures of militarisation. While the geostrategic weights represent military potential, measures of militarisation give some indication as to the ability and will of each state to translate economic and human potential into building a military establishment.

The chapter will then discuss measures of military capability. Three different balances will be dealt with in detail: first, the balance between Iran and Iraq; second, the balance between Iraq and Saudi Arabia; and third, the balance between Iraq and the GCC states as a whole. Ground forces play the central role in all three balances, supported by airpower and these categories will be the focus of analysis. Naval forces are excluded since they would have a marginal impact on these balances. A fourth balance is also addressed, albeit briefly. This is the air and naval balance between Iran and Saudi Arabia/GCC.

Two approaches will be employed in assessing military balances: first, the quantitative equipment balance will be analysed by 'bean-counting,' i.e. simply adding up equipment holdings in different

Military Capability

categories; and second, a quantitative net assessment model will be employed. This model is based on the Weapon Effectiveness Index/Weighted Unit Value (WEI/WUV) approach. This involves assigning numerical values to types of weaponry in order to calculate a numerically quantifiable balance. Although this model has its flaws, it does at least provide a method of aggregating disparate weapons systems and comparing different force structures.

Geostrategic weights

In order to place the military balance in context it is useful to look at the fundamentals of geostrategic power. Although there is much discussion in international relations today of a shift to geo-economics and the decline of the utility of traditional measures of national power, in the Gulf the traditional criteria are still relevant as it is something of a Hobbesian environment.[1] This assessment focuses on 'hard' measures of national power that can be translated directly in military might rather than on soft measures such as cultural influence.

The tables in Appendix 1 plot population and GDP in the Gulf states from 1975 to 1995. They highlight the naturally dominant position of Iran in terms of population, 64.8 million in 1995 compared to 21 million for Iraq and 18.6 million for Saudi Arabia.[2] On the Arabian Peninsula, the total GCC population in 1995 was 24.94 million, greater than Iraq's. It should be noted, though, that the actual strength of the GCC states in terms of population is overestimated by these figures because of the large proportion of expatriates in their population. For instance, expatriates make up some 30 per cent of the Saudi total and up to 80 per cent of the UAE total. In most cases, these populations would add little to the strategic weight of their host nations.[3]

In regard to GDP it must be noted that the figures are even more unreliable, especially for the Iranian and Iraqi economies due to the problems of collecting statistics and of exchange rate calculations.[4]

Furthermore, Iraq's impoverished state since 1990 as a result of UN sanctions must be taken into account. Although the Iraqi economy will take a long time to recover, it retains significant medium term potential.[5]

In order to reduce the impact of these statistical problems, it is useful to look at GDP figures over time. In 1990, the leading position of Saudi Arabia was clear ($88bn) compared to Iran's $60bn and Iraq's $41bn. By 1995, Saudi Arabia's lead was even more striking at $128bn, compared to Iran's stagnant economy which generated only $60bn and Iraq's collapsing economy which had an estimated GDP of $18.5bn. The UAE and Kuwait were clearly leading powers in terms of GDP, with $36.7bn and $25.4bn respectively in 1995. Bahrain, Oman and Qatar had GDPs of between $4.6bn and $12bn in 1995. It is interesting to note that, in 1995, the combined GDPs of the six GCC states totalled $214.7bn, over three and a half times that of Iran or over five times the size of Iraq's economy in 1990.

In sum, in the Iran-Iraq balance, Iran clearly has the advantage in terms of both population (almost three times the Iraqi total) and GDP. In terms of population, Iran also looms over the GCC states, though they far outstrip it in terms of GDP. Saudi Arabia and Kuwait together are marginally weaker than Iraq in terms of total population but tower over it in terms of GDP.

Relative militarisation

Although total population and aggregate wealth are significant factors in the strategic balance, it is necessary to examine the extent to which different societies have converted these inputs into military outputs. This can be done by looking at total defence expenditures and then converting these figures into per capita defence spending and defence spending as a proportion of GDP. In addition, the force ratios of standing military personnel to the population as a whole have been calculated to arrive at a non-monetary estimate of the defence burden.

Military Capability

These calculations give an indication of the defence burden that countries choose to bear and the relative emphasis they place on military spending.[6] The relevant figures are tabulated in Appendix 2.

In terms of total defence expenditure it is unsurprising that both Iran and Iraq spent heavily during the mid-1980s in the course of their war. Iranian spending rose to $14bn in 1985 compared to Iraq's $12.9bn. By 1990 Iran's spending had dropped off sharply, to $3.18bn but Iraq's remained high at $8.6bn. By 1995 both countries' spending had fallen to around $2.5bn. Saudi Arabia's defence spending has been consistently high and has not fallen significantly over the past five years, remaining at $13.2bn in 1995. Spending by the other five GCC states has also increased steadily and, in 1995, totalled $7.3bn.

As for the burden imposed by defence spending, in terms of per capita expenditure, it is striking that Saudi Arabia scores consistently highest out of the three main powers. Per capita defence spending in Iran fell from $312 in 1985 to $38 in 1995 while in Iraq it fell from $836 in 1985 to $128 in 1995. In Saudi Arabia, however, per capita defence spending reached $1525 per person in 1985 and fell to around $709 in 1995.[7] Only the smaller GCC states have matched this figure. Oman and the UAE spent $1010 and $1027 per head in 1995 while Kuwait spent a massive $1927 per person.

The picture is rather different when expressed in terms of defence spending as a proportion of GDP. Here, Iraq leads the way. During the 1980s it strove to match Iran's military might and, in 1985, was spending a colossal 57 per cent of GDP on defence. This fell in the late 1980s but, in 1990, the figure was still around 21.1 per cent, by which time the Iranian burden had fallen to a mere 5.4 per cent. Saudi Arabia's large GDP has enabled it to spend heavily on defence without burdening itself to this extent and the proportion has fallen since 1975 as the economy has expanded. In 1975 the defence burden was over 27 per cent but by 1995 it had fallen to just over 10 per cent.

Kuwait, spending 11.4 per cent, and Oman, spending 15.9 per cent, were the only regional states with such high burdens in 1995. Bahrain, Qatar and the UAE all entered the mid-1990s with defence burdens of between 4.2 and 5.5 per cent.

It is also useful to look at force ratios in order to estimate the defence burden in manpower terms. Again, these have changed over time. In 1985, Iran reached a level of 23.3 (standing military manpower per 1000 inhabitants) and Iraq a level of 54.9, reflecting Iraq's higher mobilisation and greater commitment to war against its larger neighbour. By 1990 the ratios had fallen to 9.8 for Iran and 19.3 for Iraq. They have changed little since. Interestingly, Saudi Arabia's ratio went from 5.8 in 1985 to 10.5 in 1990 to 8.7 in 1995. These relatively low figures highlight the fact that the Kingdom has followed a capital rather than a manpower intensive approach to force building. The proportion in the smaller Gulf states is higher and ranges from (in 1995) 11 in Kuwait to 38.3 in the UAE. These figures reflect the fact that, in such small countries, fielding even a small military force requires a significant commitment of personnel.[8]

To conclude, these figures for relative militarisation reinforce in a statistical sense the conventional wisdom about the military balance in the Gulf. The GCC states have on the whole relied on a capital intensive approach to force building which has involved high total and per capita expenditure. This spending has not, however, constituted a major burden on their expanding economies, with the notable exception of Oman.[9] Iran and Iraq, in contrast, have relied on higher mobilisation rates and on building large armed forces on which proportionately less is spent. Iraq's smaller population and economy have, however, made the financial and human burden of defence harder to bear than for Iran.

Two interesting observations of possible future import can be added. First, Iran's light defence burden, compared to Iraq, suggests that it has considerable potential to invest in a large scale military build-up.

Second, Saudi Arabia has a much lower force ratio than its GCC partners. While recognising that each country's situation is unique, one could conclude that it may not be impossible for Saudi Arabia to increase the size of its armed forces by adopting similar force ratios to those of its neighbours. If the Kingdom merely equalled Kuwait's force ratio, then it could deploy total armed forces of almost 205 000 men, adding over 40 000 men to its current forces.

Military capability

The measures used above give insight into different facets of the strategic equation but the core of this research is concerned with actual and projected military capabilities. Methods of assessing military capabilities and balances range from the straightforward totting up of totals of equipment, units or personnel to mathematically sophisticated simulations and war games of hypothetical battles and campaigns factoring in hardware quantity and quality as well as troop quality, C^3I abilities and logistical and doctrinal elements, and political events.

A basic distinction in such analyses is between static assessments of pre-battle inputs and dynamic models that predict battle outputs, or the results of conflicts.[10] Static assessments provide only a rough guide to the military balance. Viewed historically, they are poor predictors of the outcome of a conflict as many other factors intervene between the quantitative input and victory or defeat. Dynamic assessments attempt to go a stage further and model a conflict in order to determine the likely outcome.[11] There are numerous methodologies that have been used for this process. One may be called 'operational,' relying on military principles, doctrines, terrain and historical experience.[12] Another is formal mathematical modelling using one of a variety of models, often based on the Lanchester equations.[13] A third method is war-gaming, which combines modelling with free play. These techniques have all been used extensively in the US defence analytical community since the

Second World War, if with varying degrees of acceptance. The former USSR probably went furthest in the development of these techniques, combining static assessments based on equipment trials with quantifications of operational factors derived from the Red Army's experiences in the Second World War.

Dynamic modelling of potential future conflicts in the Gulf is an extremely valuable approach. It is used extensively by official bodies such as CENTCOM. Such work has not yet been attempted by researchers working in the public domain but it is to be hoped that this will change in the future.[14] As a first step, this section presents a static assessment of the military balance of power. Two techniques are used: first, 'bean-counting' of equipment holdings; second, the WEI/WUV net assessment methodology which allows for aggregate quantification of ground force balances. When engaging in this sort of accounting, however, one must be careful not to overestimate its utility. As prominent US defence analyst Eliot Cohen warned, 'net assessment has a number of functions. It gives us a sense of what might occur should war in fact break out. It should also help us to understand peacetime processes of competition.' [15] It does not, however, claim to predict the outcome of a confrontation.

Bean counting

This is the classic way to assess military balances. It was used throughout the Cold War in official and media reporting of the East-West confrontation and is used now in the Gulf among governments and the media. Its attraction is that it is simple and intuitive. However, it is widely recognised that, by itself, it is no real basis on which to judge a military balance, let alone the likely outcome of a confrontation. As one critic of the method put it, "bean counts' ... do not constitute assessments of comparative warfighting capability ... They are mere static accountings of prebattle inputs.'[16]

Military Capability

Such a static accounting does, however, at least provide a starting point for measuring the balance. The data on which the comparisons are made is tabulated in Appendix 3 while accompanying charts show balances for certain categories and the evolution of these balances over time.[17] The figures have been derived from a combination of sources as outlined in the introduction. Details of present and future holdings for each country have been discussed in the preceding chapters.

A point of departure is to look at military manpower levels, both total and standing. It should be emphasised that aggregate manpower levels are a poor indicator of military capability but they nonetheless need to be mentioned since they are a commonly used measure of relative strength. In 1995, Iran's standing manpower was 630 000 compared to Iraq's 382 500. Although Iran's standing forces are almost 65 per cent more numerous than Iraq's, when reserves are taken into account, then Iraq's forces outnumber Iran's by five per cent (1 032 500 to 983 000).[18]

In 1995, Saudi Arabia could muster some 162 500 regulars and 20 000 reservists.[19] The other GCC states could muster 151 900 regulars in 1995, the bulk from the UAE (70 000) and Oman (43 500). Iraq's standing forces therefore outnumbered Saudi Arabia's by almost two and a half times and outnumbered total GCC manpower by over 20 per cent.

Although these manpower levels give some indication of the relative sizes of the Gulf states' military establishments, they are, as noted, of limited interest. As both the Iran-Iraq War and the Gulf War demonstrated, military hardware is likely to count for more than mass manpower in any future confrontation. Five categories of equipment will be examined here: MBTs, Other Armoured Fighting Vehicles (OAFVs), artillery, armed helicopters and combat aircraft.

The Tank Balance

Iran and Iraq have consistently dominated the MBT balance in the Gulf since the 1970s. The balance between the two shifted radically from 1975 when the ratio was 1.05 in Iran's favour to 1985 when it was 4.5 in *Iraq's* favour. By 1995, Iraq's advantage over Iran had fallen to 1.87. By 2000, Iraq's advantage will fall to a marginal 1.1. Assuming no major Iraqi imports, Iran's force building programme will almost have equalised the balance by the end of the decade. (Chart 1) This shift is even more striking if we include only advanced MBTs.[20] The dramatic imbalance between a force equipped with, for instance, Abrams M1s, and, for instance, T-55/62s, was demonstrated during the Gulf War when US armoured units were able to engage and destroy Iraqi armoured units almost with impunity.[21] Whereas in 1995 Iraq had some 300 advanced MBTs compared to Iran's 225, by the year 2000 Iran's fleet of T-72s will outnumber Iraq's T-72 force by over three times.

In the meantime, Saudi Arabia and the other GCC states are substantially reinforcing their MBT holdings. Saudi Arabia had some 450 MBTs in 1985 but had increased this to 1035 by 1995. It is likely to have 1075 by the year 2000 and 1125 five years later. This expansion means that Iraq's current numerical superiority of 2.27 times will fall to 2.1 by the year 2005. (Chart 2) More importantly, Saudi Arabia's investment in modern MBTs at a time when Iraq is denied such equipment means that the Kingdom's current advantage in this category will rise from a ratio of 2.5 to 3.8 by the year 2005.

The other GCC states are also expanding and modernising their armoured forces. From a level of some 100 in 1975, they now own 602 MBTs. This is likely to rise to 1069 in the year 2000 and 1191 by 2005. As with Saudi Arabia, they are acquiring modern MBTs. Over the next decade most of their older tanks should be replaced by advanced MBTs. The total combined GCC tank force will come to almost match Iraq's in quantity, while greatly superseding it in terms of quality. By the year 2005, Iraq will still have marginally more tanks than the GCC, by a ratio of 1.1, but the GCC's force of

Military Capability

advanced MBTs will outnumber Iraq's by over seven and a half times (Chart 3).

Other Armoured Fighting Vehicles

Other Armoured Fighting Vehicles include AIFVs, APCs and ARVs. The newer AIFVs are important in their own right as fighting vehicles but the older APCs and troop carriers are important as an indicator of the ability of mechanised infantry to operate with armoured units. For the sake of simplicity, all types are grouped together in this category. On the Iran-Iraq front, Iraq has consistently dominated the balance. In 1995 Iraq still had some 4400 OAFVs while Iran had a mere 965. Iran is acquiring more OAFVs but its infantry will continue to suffer from a lack of mobility compared to Iraq. Over the next decade, Iraq's superiority in this category will fall significantly but not crucially from a ratio of 4.6 to 2.76.

Since the mid-1980s, Saudi Arabia's efforts to develop mechanised infantry forces, especially the National Guard, have meant that it now holds more of these vehicles than Iraq. Saudi Arabia's holdings have increased from 1550 in 1985 to 4005 in 1995. This total is set to increase, meaning that the ratio will change from 1.1 in Iraq's favour to 1.13 in Saudi Arabia's favour by the year 2005.

Acquisitions in the other GCC states will likewise tip the balance against Iraq, though the holdings of OAFVs in the smaller GCC states are marginal compared to Saudi Arabia. Total OAFV holdings in the GCC will rise from 5912 in 1995 to 7494 in 2005, giving the GCC a 1.7 superiority over Iraq in this category.

Artillery

Iraq relied heavily on artillery in the war against Iran and, in 1985, its 5270 artillery tubes (towed and self-propelled) outnumbered Iran's in a ratio of 8.8. The Gulf War, however, decimated Iraq's artillery holdings and Iran now dominates with 2884 against Iraq's 1730. By the year 2000, the ratio is set to shift further in Iran's favour to 1.7. A similar story can be told about MRLs. In 1985 Iraq had 200 to Iran's 65 but by 1995 Iran had 425 and Iraq 250. By 2000, the ratio is set to be at least 1.8 in Iran's favour.

Saudi Arabia and the GCC states remain far behind Iraq in terms of artillery holdings. Iraq holds over 4.4 times as many artillery pieces as Saudi Arabia, a ratio that is likely to persist for the next decade. Iraq also has more than four times as many MRLs as Saudi Arabia. This advantage will decline somewhat by 2005, to two and a half times. If total GCC holdings are taken into account, Iraq's current superiority in artillery of 2.19 will fall marginally to 2.18 over the coming decade. Iraq's superiority in MRLs will fall more significantly from 1995's ratio of 2.1 to 1.3.

Armed Helicopters

Armed helicopters are an increasingly important part of regional arsenals. Iraq employed them extensively in the Iran-Iraq War and Iranian officials have even hinted that they believe they have superseded the tank. The GCC states were impressed by their performance in the Gulf War and several have launched major acquisition programmes. Although helicopters are unlikely to be directly ranged against each other, counting them gives an indication of the close air support that armoured and mechanised forces are likely to enjoy.

Iran and Iraq now have similar numbers (105 and 123 respectively). Unless either country proceeds with as yet unannounced acquisitions or domestic production, these totals are unlikely to change over the coming decade. The introduction of large numbers of sophisticated gunships into the GCC forces is of more importance, especially given the likely nature of any future Iraqi armoured threat to Kuwait or Saudi Arabia. Although they have had problems operating and

Military Capability

purchasing new helicopters, several of the GCC states are determined to increase their holdings. Although Saudi Arabia is purchasing new aircraft, Iraq will retain a superiority in this category, falling from a ratio of 4.6 in 1995 to 2.4 in 2005. Acquisitions in other GCC states will however tip the overall Iraqi-GCC ratio from 1.2 in Iraq's favour in 1995 to 1.4 in the GCC's favour by the year 2005.

Fixed-Wing Combat Aircraft

Although this study concentrates on the ground balance, and so will consider the impact of air power in terms of close air support, the combat aircraft balance is of much wider significance than merely in terms of what it adds to the ground force balance. The geography of the Gulf, mainly open desert on the Arabian Peninsula and waterways separating Iran from its southern neighbours, means that airpower will be a leading, perhaps decisive, arm in any future confrontations. Even more so than with ground forces, a quantitative comparison of platforms is a poor guide to the balance in the air. Quality of aircraft, avionics, weapons systems, training, maintenance facilities and C^3I are of more importance than numbers. An integrated assessment of these factors is beyond the scope of this study. Nonetheless, a simple comparison of the numbers of aircraft highlights some important trends in the balance.

The evolution of the balance highlights the collapse of the Iranian Air Force in the early 1980s, from 317 serviceable combat aircraft in 1975 to 70 in 1985 and the expansion of the Iraqi Air Force in the same period, from 299 to 500 aircraft. The Gulf War, however, tipped the balance back towards Iran. By 1995 Iraq had some 341 aircraft while Iran had 390. If current acquisition plans are fulfilled, then Iran's superiority will rise to a ratio of 1.3 in 2000 and 1.6 in 2005. (Chart 4) A more important measure is the number of advanced combat aircraft. In this category the degradation of the Iraqi Air Force and the modernisation of the Iranian Air Force is even more dramatic. Iran and Iraq now have similar numbers of advanced combat aircraft (158 and 160 respectively). By the end of the decade Iran will have 212 to Iraq's 160 and by 2005 Iran will have 292 such aircraft, or 1.8 times as many as Iraq.

The growth of Saudi airpower is even more striking. From 97 combat aircraft in 1975, the Saudi Air Force grew to 264 in 1995. By 2005 the RSAF should have 302 aircraft. This would reduce Iraq's superiority from a ratio of 1.3 to 1.1. (Chart 5) More importantly, over the next ten years the deployment of advanced combat aircraft by Saudi Arabia will mean that the RSAF will far outclasses Iraq's antiquated air force. Both countries now have roughly equal holdings of advanced aircraft but the RSAF will enjoy an advantage of 1.5 times by the year 2000, rising to 1.8 five years later.

The expansion and modernisation of Saudi airpower is being matched by developments in the other GCC air forces which will tilt the balance further. At present, total GCC holdings of combat aircraft outnumber Iraq's by a ratio of 1.4. Over the next ten years this ratio will increase to 1.5. (Chart 6) More importantly, the GCC's current 1.7 advantage in advanced aircraft will increase to 2.6 times by the year 2005.

The Iran-Saudi/GCC Balance

As long as southern Iraq remains under Baghdad's control, there is no real prospect of a confrontation between Iranian and GCC ground forces. The most that could occur would be a limited Iranian amphibious incursion into a southern Gulf state. In light of this, this study makes no attempt to assess the balance of ground forces between Iran and the GCC states. However, it is worth examining the changing balance in air and naval forces. Modelling this balance would require techniques not used here, so it will have to suffice to use bean-counting.

Military Capability

In any future conventional clash between Iran and the GCC states it would be airpower that would bear the brunt of the battle. Currently, Iran has significantly more combat aircraft than Saudi Arabia, 390 compared to 264. The GCC as a whole, however, outnumber Iran, with 486 aircraft. The GCC's advantageous ratio of 1.25 is set to become negative by the year 2005, when Iran will have 1.04 times as many combat aircraft as the combined GCC states.

In air battles above the Gulf, or in the context of strikes on one anothers' territories, however, only the latest aircraft are likely to be of any real value. In terms of advanced aircraft, by 2005 Saudi Arabia's current marginal advantage of 1.03 is likely to turn into an Iranian advantage of around 1.03. If all GCC air forces are combined, then the GCC's current advantageous ratio of 1.7 will decline to 1.4 over the next decade. The current balances demonstrate why Iran feels threatened by its current inferiority in this arena, especially when Western air power in the region is added to the air threat faced by Tehran. However, the predicted ratios these ratios highlight is the threat to the GCC posed by Iran's arms build up in the air. Although the growing Iranian strength in platforms may be offset by GCC investment in stand-off weapons, Iran's growing arsenal of SSMs must be added to the air threat faced by the GCC states.

Assessing the naval balance is difficult because Iran's adoption of an unconventional strategy makes comparison of major surface or subsurface platforms of limited use. Iran's two or three destroyers have no equivalent in the GCC navies, neither do its two, soon to be three, submarines. Iran has three frigates, compared to eight in the Saudi Navy. By the year 2005, the GCC navies will have 18 frigates. Iran has two corvettes compared to the GCC's four; in a decade the GCC should have six. Iran's 10 missile craft currently face 30 in the GCC navies; they will face 34 by 2005. In terms of fast attack craft, Iran now has 71 and is likely to increase to some 85 in ten years time. The GCC will have around 36 by then. The GCC's current advantage in armed naval helicopters is likely to increase over the next decade but this may be offset by Iran's deployment of anti-ship missiles based on islands, oil platforms and small boats.

In sum, it is hard to assess the GCC-Iran naval balance through numbers alone. It seems likely that the GCC forces will have only a limited ability to protect installations and shipping against Iranian guerrilla tactics. Considering their training patterns, they will also have only limited ability to take offensive action against Iranian installations.

Bean Counting Conclusion

In relation to the Iran-Iraq balance, the projected figures tell a clear story. Iran is outstripping Iraq's armed forces in most categories. Iraq will retain an advantage in OAFVs and armed helicopters, but is falling behind in terms of MBTs, artillery and combat aircraft. More importantly, Iran is set to completely outclass Iraq in the areas of advanced MBTs and advanced combat aircraft. Having seen in the Gulf War what a difference modern equipment can make if well handled, Iraq's generals must be badly worried by the evolving balance of forces.

In terms of the Saudi/GCC-Iraq balance, the differential is not so stark but the GCC's force building plans are redressing previous Iraqi superiority. Saudi Arabia and the GCC states remain dramatically weaker in numbers of artillery pieces and MRLs. The balance in helicopters is ambiguous, depending on whether one counts just Saudi Arabia or adds in the smaller GCC states. In terms of MBTs and combat aircraft, though, the GCC states are redressing the balance, especially if quality is taken into account. Saudi Arabia will come to outnumber Iraq in terms of advanced tanks, but will remain unable to match Iraq's overall mass. If all GCC states are combined, then Iraq's lead in older MBTs becomes irrelevant and its tank forces will be further outclassed as each year passes. In the air, the growing GCC advantage is equally striking. By itself, Saudi Arabia is

Military Capability

becoming ever more dominant, Iraq's large arsenal of older aircraft notwithstanding. If all GCC aircraft are combined, then Iraq's air force ceases to be a significant challenge.

Net assessment

Bean-counting is of only limited utility as a guide to the balance of military inputs since it compares like with like instead of assessing how the different parts of a combined armed force will work together. A more useful approach is to aggregate different types of equipment to arrive at a total value which can be compared directly with an opposing force. Such techniques often use a combination of quantifiable aspects of equipment performance, such as firepower, mobility and protection and subjective judgments by a survey group of experts regarding the relative weights to be given to categories of equipment. One methodology was developed by The Analytic Sciences Corporation and incorporates air and ground forces in its net assessment.[22] The methodology has, however, not been made public and so cannot be used here.

The methodology used in this study is one that focuses primarily on ground forces. It was developed by the US government in the 1970s. It involves giving each weapon an effectiveness rating (Weapon Effectiveness Indices or WEI) and multiplying it by a category weight to reach a Weighted Unit Value (WUV). The scores are then normalised by comparing them to a US armoured division for the sake of comparison. Strengths are expressed in Armoured Division Equivalents (ADE).[23]

This method has a number of problems. As Cohen warned, 'no sensible ... conductor would attempt to evaluate the instruments in the orchestra according to a common index of musical effectiveness. Yet the ADE enforces just this kind of absurdity. ... [Nonetheless] the ADE does indeed have some usefulness as an accounting measure—a look at ADE scores over time provides some useful information about the development of opposing forces in peacetime.'[24] A practical problem with applying the technique is that the data available in the public domain is not applicable to the most modern weaponry. Although scholars have applied the technique to third world states in the 1990s they have been hampered by this lacuna.[25] This study will follow their lead in making what seem like reasonable extrapolations from old figures to account for more modern equipment. These extrapolations have, however, been kept on the conservative side.

As with the bean counting method, net assessment calculations have been carried out for three different balances over the next decade. First, the Iran-Iraq balance. Second, the Iraq-Saudi Arabia balance. Third, the Iraq-GCC balance. In all cases the simplifying assumption has been made that all of each states forces are committed so figures are calculated for aggregate national military capability. Clearly this is an unrealistic assumption since there are virtually no conceivable scenarios in which this assumption would hold. Even if Iran and Iraq were to engage in all out war, they would hold back forces to counter threats from other neighbours. The same holds true of Saudi Arabia which would at least maintain forces on the Yemeni front in any future confrontation with Iraq. This holds even more true for the other GCC states, none of whom would willingly send all their forces to help fight off an Iraqi attack on Kuwait or Saudi Arabia. Nonetheless, this simplifying assumption is made since the purpose of this study is to discern broad strategic trends rather than to war-game hypothetical conflicts.

For each balance, two different calculations have been carried out.[26] First, just aggregate ground forces are included. These scores include all army combat equipment—MBTs, ARV, AIFV, APC, artillery and MRLs, mortars, ATGWs and RCL. In addition, 10 per cent of standing man power is counted as bearing small arms in the front line.[27]

Second, close air support (CAS) is factored into the equation.[28] On the Iran-Iraq front it is assumed that neither country's air force dominates the air space, meaning that each sides' CAS, fixed wing and rotary wing, is free to operate over the battlefield. This may, though, underestimate the growing ability of the Iranian Air Force to carry out interdiction and strike operations inside Iraq. On the Saudi-Iraq and GCC-Iraq fronts, it is assumed that Saudi Arabia and the GCC dominate the air space, if not attaining air superiority over Iraq. While Saudi and GCC CAS operates at full strength, it is assumed that half of Iraq's CAS is prevented from operating. The method used for calculating the impact of CAS is derived from Posen, *Inadvertent Escalation*.[29]

In subsequent iterations of the model, an attempt has been made to account for 'soft' factors such as logistics and C^3I. This calculation is carried out only for the balances including Iraq, Saudi Arabia, and the GCC states since it is assumed that Iran and Iraq have similar capabilities in these areas. Although a number of dynamic modelling approaches attempt to quantify these elements, as well as others such as morale, training and doctrine, the incorporation of such factors is notoriously controversial. Even more than with the other applications of the model, then, this assessment should be regarded as no more than an indication of possible advantages accruing from investment in these areas.

This recalculation takes two forms. First, the calculation attempts to take account of maintenance and reliability issues. At present, and for the medium term, Iran and Iraq face serious reliability problems with their armoured vehicles, especially with their older MBTs. Saudi Arabia and the GCC states also face reliability problems and are hampered by a shortage of maintenance personnel, forcing them to rely on foreign contractors. Nonetheless, their maintenance problems do not appear as severe as those faced by Iran and Iraq. Taking account of this factor reflects the higher Saudi and GCC investment in logistics and support.[30]

Second, the ADE balance is recalculated adding in a notional multiplier to reflect Saudi Arabia's higher investment in C^3I and logistics as a whole. The approach here is similar to that followed by Posen, who argued that NATO's high tail to teeth ratio should act as a force multiplier in combat.[31] The addition of this multiplier is not meant to suggest that the Saudi Arabia's investment in these areas *will* pay off so handsomely, merely to examine what the balance would look like *if* this investment did act as a significant force multiplier.[32] The calculation is carried out only for Saudi Arabia since it is assumed that problems with integrating command and control among GCC states would negate any multiplier effect.

The Iran—Iraq Balance

The Iran-Iraq force ratio measured in ADEs is illustrated in Chart 7. At present the two states' armed forces are roughly equal with Iran having a marginal, but insignificant advantage. Over the next four years, however, Iran's lead is set to widen significantly. By the year 2000 the Iran:Iraq force ratio could be 1.25. Barring any major further arms acquisitions by either side, this balance is likely to persist for the next decade.

Factoring in CAS makes little difference to the balance since both countries have similar CAS assets. Assuming a two week battle, Iran loses 0.666 ADE from Iraqi CAS while Iraq loses 0.654 ADE from Iranian air attacks. The CAS battle helps Iran improve its position marginally, boosting its ratio to 1.26 in the year 2000 and beyond.

The Iraq—Saudi Arabia Balance

The Iraq-Saudi Arabia balance is illustrated in Chart 8. The significant growth in Saudi Arabia's combat potential is noticeable. In 1995 the Iraq:Saudi ground force ratio was 1.62. By 2000 this should narrow to 1.34 and five years later it may be 1.22. This leaves Iraq with a significant advantage but not an overwhelming one.

Factoring in CAS is a net benefit to Saudi Arabia. Whereas Saudi Arabia loses 0.196 ADE to Iraqi CAS, Iraqi losses measure 0.49 ADE in 1995, 0.366 ADE in 2000 and 0.55 ADE in the year 2005. This positive exchange ratio for Saudi Arabia brings down the aggregate Iraq:Saudi force ratio to 1.59 in 1995, 1.32 in 2000 and 1.19 in 2005. While not decisive, these figures reflect an advantage for Saudi CAS.

The third line in Chart 8 demonstrates the effect of including some assumptions about higher Saudi MBT reliability rates on the ground force balance (excluding CAS). Although Saudi Arabia has maintenance problems, these are minor in comparison with the problems Iraq faces. Under these assumptions, Iraq's advantage slips from a ratio of 1.35 in 1995 to 1.1 in 2000 while the force ratio tends towards equality by the year 2005.

The fourth line on Chart 8, labelled Saudi optimistic, is designed to illustrate the hypothetical force balance if all of Saudi Arabia's advantages are counted in. This represents the aggregate force ratio if ground forces, CAS and higher Saudi MBT reliability rates are included. Furthermore, a multiplier of 1.2 has been applied to the Saudi ground strength in order to reflect higher investment in C^3I and logistics. In this example, Iraq's marginal advantage of 1.08 in 1995 declines to 0.89 in 2000 and 0.79 in the year 2005. In other words, Saudi Arabia *alone* is more than a match for Iraq by the end of the decade.

The Iraq—GCC Balance

The Iraq—GCC balance is illustrated in Chart 9. The chart combines the ADE totals for Saudi Arabia and its GCC partners. In practice such military coordination in a crisis is highly unlikely but the figures nonetheless demonstrate the striking growth of the GCC's military potential compared to Iraq. Whereas in 1995 Iraq had a slight advantage over the GCC to the ratio of 1.02, by the end of the decade the ratio shifts to 1.32 in the GCC's favour. Five years later the GCC's advantage rises to 1.42.

Taking air support into account, the GCC's growing advantage is even more marked. The GCC forces lose 0.196 ADE from Iraqi CAS in all cases but Iraq's losses mount from 1.065 ADE in 1995 to 1.325 ADE in 2005. This shifts the force ratios in the GCC's favour from 1995 on. In 1995 the GCC's superiority is 1.07, in 2000 it will rise to 1.47 and in 2005 will become 1.6.

The third line on Chart 9 demonstrates the effect of including some assumptions regarding MBT reliability rates on the ground force balance (excluding CAS). Immediately the combined GCC forces have an advantage of 1.18, rising to 1.6 in 2000 and 1.74 in the year 2005.

Net assessment conclusion

The aggregate force ratios calculated above are only one factor in assessing pre-battle inputs and so only one element in judging relative military strengths. The calculations refer to the whole of each nation's ground forces and CAS but, in operational terms, the important question is how able each country is to mass forces and achieve local superiority at the decisive strategic point, rather than on whether the country as a whole has powerful armed forces. This question can only be answered with reference to terrain, operational doctrine and a variety of other factors. Nonetheless, the total force ratios analysed above do give an indication of trends in the military balance of power.

In terms of the Iran- Iraq balance, the ADE force ratio demonstrates that the balance is shifting markedly in Iran's favour. Although the two countries are roughly at parity at present, the projected strengthening of Iran's ground forces over the coming four to five years should give it a significant advantage. Close air support makes

Military Capability

little difference to the balance since both sides have similar capabilities. The model used here does not, however, take account of other aspects of air power such as long range strike and interdiction. Iran's growing fleet of advanced strike aircraft and SSMs may help it shift the balance further in its favour.

The Iraq-Saudi balance is also shifting. Considering just ground forces, the Iraqi superiority is set to decline over the coming decade if Saudi Arabia expands its army and National Guard and builds up its armoured and mechanised units. Iraq will remain the more powerful but a force ratio of merely 1.2:1 by the year 2005 does not give it a decisive superiority. Saudi investments in airpower will help tip the balance further over the next decade. It is striking that CAS makes a limited impact on the balance. This is partly because Saudi Arabia is not investing heavily in CAS assets but instead in air superiority and strike aircraft. It is likely that the latter would tip the balance further in the Kingdom's favour. Giving Saudi Arabia credit for its investment in logistics and C^3I is a controversial move but it can be justified in light of the fact that the Iraqi army has had problems in these areas in past campaigns and is not able to match the Kingdom's investment in high-technology management, communications and technical intelligence assets. Granted these assumptions, it is striking that Saudi Arabia could, in theory, look forward to matching Iraq's forces over the next decade.

The GCC-Iraq balance is more of a notional one included for illustrative purposes. For the foreseeable future there is little likelihood of the armed forces of the GCC states being willing or able to operate together against an external threat. Despite political statements of intent and years of advice from their Western allies, the GCC states remain divided by political and dynastic rivalries. They have even been unable to coordinate a joint air defence network in the Gulf, surely a prerequisite to closer coordination.[33] Nonetheless, the calculations presented above demonstrate what a powerful force the GCC states could be if they were to cooperate. In terms of their equipment holdings, the GCC states will be more than a match for Iraq by the end of the decade. If they are given credit for their investment in CAS and/or higher maintenance efforts, then the balance could shift markedly in their favour over the next five to ten years.

Notes

1. E. Luttwak, 'The Global Setting of US Military Power,' in L. B. Ederington and M.J. Mazarr, eds., *Turning Point: The Gulf War and U.S. Military Strategy* (Boulder, CO, Westview Press, 1994), pp. 3-22.
2. There is considerable uncertainty regarding these figures, especially with regard to Saudi Arabia. The consensus of demographers appears to be that Saudi Arabia consistently overestimates its national and total populations in order to make itself appear stronger in relation to Yemen.
3. This is not, of course, to diminish the vital economic role played by these expatriates.
4. J. Amuzegar, *Iran's Economy Under the Islamic Republic* (London, I.B. Tauris, 1993), pp. viii-x.
5. A. Alnasrawi, 'What Economic Future for Iraq?', *Middle East Executive Reports*, March 1996, pp. 8 & 13-19.
6. In view of the difficulties inherent in estimating GDP and defence budgets in these states, these monetary calculations only represent very rough estimates. In particular, Iran's defence budget may be underestimated as official figures exclude a number of major categories. Saudi Arabia's, in contrast, may be over-estimated since it involves a range of non-military costs.
7. This is probably, however, only a statistical anomaly caused by the sudden rise in reported Saudi population in the 1995 figures.
8. It should also be noted that, in many of these states, employment in the military, as in the civil service, serves a social welfare function. In addition, the employment of large numbers of expatriates in the armed forces of some of these states, notably the UAE, skews the figures somewhat.
9. World Bank, *Sultanate of Oman: Sustainable Growth and Economic Diversification*, 31 May 1994, report No. 12199-OM, p. 66.
10. For this distinction, see: S.D. Biddle, 'The European conventional balance: A reinterpretation of the debate,' *Survival*, March/April, 1988, pp. 99-121.
11. B.R. Posen, 'Is NATO Decisively Outnumbered?' *International Security*, Vol. 12, No. 4 (Spring 1988), pp. 186-202.

12. Mearsheimer, 'Numbers, Strategy, and the European Balance', *International Security*.
13. A prominent critic of the Lanchester equations and proponent of an alternative dynamic model is Joshua Epstein. J.M. Epstein, *The Calculus of Conventional War: Dynamic Analysis without Lanchester Theory* (Washington, DC, Brookings, 1985). For discussion of another model, see: J.D. Steinbrunner and L.V. Sigal, eds., *Alliance Security: NATO and the No-First-Use Question* (Washington DC, Brookings, 1983), pp. 208-216.
14. An interesting attempt to model a US-Soviet confrontation in the Gulf is detailed in J.M. Epstein, *Strategy & Force Planning: The Case of the Persian Gulf* (Washington, DC, Brookings, 1987).
15. E.A. Cohen, 'Toward Better Net Assessment,' *International Security*, Vol 13, No. 1 (Summer 1988), pp. 50-89.
16. J.M. Epstein, 'Dynamic Analysis and the Conventional Balance in Europe,' *International Security*, Vol. 12, No. 4 (Spring 1988), pp. 154-165. For another critique, see: D.S. Lutz, *Towards a Methodology of Military Force Comparison* (Baden-Baden, Nomos Verlagsgesellschaft, n.d.).
17. Figures for numbers of divisions and brigades have been collated but are not presented here as they add little to an understanding of the balance. This is due to the tremendous differences regarding organisation of operational units and the uncertainty over roles and numbers of administrative structures, especially in the Iranian and Iraqi armies.
18. The figures for Iran do not take into account Iran's *Basij* militia but they do include the IRGC.
19. Including SANG.
20. Advanced MBT are T-72, T-80, M-84, M-60A3, Abrams M1A1/2, Leclerc, Challenger.
21. Gordon and Trainor, *The Generals' War*, pp. 390-392.
22. The 'Technique for Assessing Comparative Force Modernization' (TASCFORM) was applied to selected Middle Eastern militaries in a 1992 study and predicted relative balances up to 1996. E. Atkeson, *A Military Assessment of the Middle East, 1991-1996* (Carlisle Barracks, PA, Strategic Studies Institute, US Army War College, December 1992).
23. The classic published work on the topic is W.P. Mako, U.S. *Ground Forces and the Defense of Central Europe* (Washington DC, Brookings, 1983).
24. Cohen, 'Toward Better Net Assessment,' *International Security*.
25. S.K. Masaki, 'The Korean Question: Assessing the Military Balance,' *Security Studies*, Vol. 4, No. 2 (Winter 1994/5), pp. 365-425 and J.W.

Moore, 'An Assessment of the Iranian Military Rearmament Programme,' *Comparative Strategy*, Vol. 13 (1994), p. 371-389.

26. ADE calculations are in Appendix 4.

27. This figure is not supposed to represent the actual proportion of infantry in the armies under discussion since this proportion could not be verified. It was derived from two calculations. First, Cordesman's observation that between 53 and 58 per cent of the Saudi army's manpower is in the combat arms. The higher figure has been taken. Second, Mako's breakdown of US, French, British and French armoured and mechanised divisions revealed that from 13-41 per cent of divisional manpower were infantrymen. The high proportion was however the exception, with the median being around 18 per cent. This study has therefore assumed that 18 per cent of the 58 per cent of soldiers in the combat arms are infantry, in other words, just over 10 per cent of the total. Cordesman, *Saudi Military Forces in the 1990s: The Strategic Challenge of Continued Modernization*, p. 18; Mako, *U.S. Ground Forces and the Defense of Central Europe*, pp. 113-120.

28. CAS calculations are in Appendix 5.

29. B. Posen, *Inadvertent Escalation: Conventional War and Nuclear Risks* (Ithaca, NY, Cornell University Press, 1991), Appendix 2. See also B. Posen, 'Measuring the European Conventional Balance,' in S.E. Miller, ed., *Conventional Forces and American Defense Policy* (Princeton, NJ, Princeton University Press, 1986), pp. 79-120.

30. The reliability rates used in this calculation are based on open source estimates rather than actual readiness rates, which were not available. In practice, readiness rates would of course depend on warning times and a host of other factors. The calculation assumes 75 per cent of older Saudi and GCC MBTs (M60s, AMXs, Chieftains) are operational. It assumes that 40 per cent of Iraq's older MBTs (all but T-72s and T-62s) are operational. The remainder are assumed to be 100 per cent operational.

31. Posen, *Inadvertent Escalation: Conventional War and Nuclear Risks*, Chapter 3.

32. A caveat made necessary by Cohen's critique of Posen's use of this multiplier. Cohen, 'Toward Better Net Assessment,' *International Security*, pp. 76-77. In response to this critique, this study uses a notional multiplier of 1.2, rather than Posen's 1.5 which seems rather high.

33. Though Bahrain and Kuwait are now attempting to coordinate their air defence networks with Saudi Arabia's newly installed Peace Shield system. 'Build-up to continue despite revenue drop,' *JDW*, p. 33; 'Bahrain Puts Air Defense at Top of Upgrade List,' *Defense News*, p. 16.

CHAPTER 6
CONCLUSIONS

This paper has demonstrated that the conventional military balance in the Gulf is not static. It is set to shift markedly over the coming decade as new arms are brought into service and as the region's armed forces restructure and retrain. This evolution of the balance has strategic implications for the West, both reassuring and worrying.

As described in the narrative chapters and demonstrated by both bean counting and net assessment, the Iran-Iraq balance is changing dramatically. Whereas Iran ended the Iran-Iraq War as the weaker party, its rearmament programme will enable it to dominate Iraq in the air as well as in aggregate ground combat potential. The Iranian lead is set to increase over the next decade and will be evident in both quantitative and qualitative terms.

The balance between Iraq and Saudi Arabia is also shifting as Saudi Arabia's force building plans are implemented and Iraq remains sanctioned. Saudi Arabia's build up, both in the air and on the ground, will reduce Iraq's military lead over the next decade. Nonetheless, the Kingdom will remain unable to match Iraq's aggregate combat potential. However, if Saudi Arabia is given credit for its higher readiness rates and/or investment in force multipliers, then the force ratio tends towards equality.

If Saudi Arabia's forces are combined with the ground and close air support forces of its GCC neighbours, then Iraq's lead disappears. Over the next five to ten years the combined GCC forces will outstrip Iraq's combat potential. The differential becomes more striking if the GCC forces are given credit for higher readiness rates.

Caveats

These conclusions must be qualified by a number of caveats dealing both with methodological issues and 'real world' problems. First, it needs to be reiterated that the assessments presented here are only intended to serve as trend indicators. By no means do they seek to predict the outcomes of any future conflict. An attempt to do so would require a full campaign analysis taking account of political factors, terrain, fighting ability, morale and a host of other, often unquantifiable, factors. Nonetheless, if the aim of building up forces is deterrence, then it should be remembered that policy makers do not judge strategic balances in terms of precise ratios. The important element is the degree of uncertainty. If a potential aggressor cannot be reasonably certain of winning a conflict, then he is much less likely to start one.

On the Iran-Iraq front, the trends are clear. Barring an Iraqi rearmament programme, Iraq will slip further behind Iran's conventional might. This is likely to deter any Iraqi aggression against Iran at the same time as making Iran bolder in its dealings with Baghdad.

On the Iraq-Saudi/GCC front, there are more imponderables that may affect the balance. Some will strengthen the position of Saudi Arabia, others may weaken it. Only a few need be mentioned here. On the positive side, Saudi Arabia (and the other GCC states') investment in deep strike and interdiction capabilities will strengthen their hand. Although it may have a few SSMs left, Iraq has a very limited deep-strike capability either with missiles or aircraft and it will take a long time to build this capability once sanctions are lifted.

On the negative side, Saudi Arabia and the GCC states face two key challenges which will impede their force modernisation. First, the shortage of indigenous manpower. This problem is particularly acute

Conclusions

for Saudi Arabia and Kuwait. Both are currently acquiring more equipment than they can man with current force levels. A more specific problem is the lack of trained personnel at both ends of the spectrum—technicians to maintain advanced equipment and senior officers well versed in commanding and controlling complex operations.[1] Second, the problem of absorbing the large quantities of high technology equipment that are coming into service.[2] The GCC states face two difficulties. First, they have bought weapons from a number of different nations with the result that they face problems of compatability and integration. Second, absorbing high technology equipment poses its own strains. Even the US military had difficulty absorbing an advanced system like the Abrams M1 when it came into service.[3] As they equip themselves with ever more sophisticated armaments, the GCC states will have to deal with the peculiar problems associated with high technology machines.[4]

Implications

These caveats notwithstanding, the changing military balance should reassure the GCC states and their Western allies that their current force-building efforts are not in vain. Saudi Arabia may not be able to match Iraq by itself but it is narrowing the gap. More importantly, if the GCC states could agree on some measure of military cooperation then they would pose a credible challenge to their larger neighbours. They may well wish to rely on the Western umbrella as a securer deterrent than their own capabilities but they may not need to do so indefinitely.

The changing balance may, however, have two less welcome implications.[5] Iraq will increasingly see itself outclassed by Iran in terms of conventional combat power. It will, meanwhile, face a growing challenge from the GCC states who are deploying advanced weapons and high-technology force multipliers to which it does not have access.[6] In addition, Iraq faces potential threats from the West (Israel and Syria) and possibly the north (Turkey). How any future Iraqi government will react to this situation is an open question. In the optimistic scenario put forward by some for the future, in which a post-Saddam Iraq is ruled by democrats on good terms with all of its neighbours, foreign policy may be demilitarised. It is more likely, though, that any future Iraqi government will feel threatened by one or more of its neighbours. In response, Iraq may either engage in large scale conventional rearmament, or it may feel the need to resort to weapons of mass destruction and related delivery systems in order to deter its neighbours.[7]

Iran's responses to the changing balance will depend on its internal political evolution. In light of its own conventional military build up Iran may feel securer against a resurgent Iraq. Tehran may even be tempted to use its strategic weight in order to bully Iraq, as the Shah did in the 1970s. On its southern front, though, Iran is clearly disturbed by the GCC arms build up. Although Iran is likely to erode the GCC's advantage in the air over the next decade, it will remain the weaker party and will be unable to compete on the same technological level. Recognition of this seems to be pushing Iran to emphasise alternative strategies, notably non-conventional and unconventional. In terms of the former, Iran is taking a leaf out of Syria's book. Unable to compete with Israeli control of the air, Syria built up a retaliatory capability based round SSMs and chemical weapons.[8] Iran is likewise developing its SSM, cruise missile and chemical weapons.[9] As it falls behind further in the technological race it may be more tempted to pursue biological or nuclear weapons.[10]

At the other end of the conflict spectrum, Iran appears to be pursuing an unconventional option. Apart from its subversive and terrorist capabilities, the IRGC is building a naval guerrilla force which includes small boats, anti-ship missiles and mines. This strategy is likely to be effective for sea denial, though not for power projection. At another level, the demonstrated ability of the Iranians for unconventional warfare raises the possibility that they may try to counter the GCC's high technology militaries with high technology unconventional warfare.[11] Although there has as yet been no sign of such an Iranian capability, the GCC states and their allies need to consider the potential Iranian information warfare threat.[12]

Notes

1. Iran and Iraq, in contrast, have officers with experience of coordinating such operations.
2. A. Cordesman, 'Current Trends in Arms Sales in the Middle East,' in S. Feldman and A. Levite, eds, *Arms Control & the New Middle East Security Environment*, JCSS (Boulder, CO, Westview Press, 1994); F. Tusa, 'Getting over the agony of absorption,' *MEED*, 12 April 1996, p. 10.
3. C.C. Demchak, *Military Organizations, Complex Machines: Modernization in the US Armed Services* (London, Ithaca, 1991).
4. In particular they will have to construct, operate and protect, the 'complex, highly-interconnected, integrated informational and logistics support system' on which advanced military equipment relies. G.I. Rochlin and C.C. Demchak, 'The Gulf war: technological and organizational implications,' *Survival*, Vol. XXXIII, No. 3 (May/June 1991), pp. 260-273.
5. These reflect, in part, Sadowksi's warning that Saudi Arabia and the GCC states are 'the most pressing threat to arms control programs in the region.' Y. Sadowski, *Scuds or Butter? The Political Economy of Arms Control in the Middle East* (Washington DC, Brookings, 1993), p. x.
6. For a discussion of the impact of these force multipliers on future warfare, see: IISS, *Strategic Survey 1995/6* (London, IISS, 1996), pp. 29-40.
7. W. Seth Carus,' Proliferation and Security in Southwest Asia,' *The Washington Quarterly*, Vol. 17, No. 2 (1994), pp. 129-139.
8. H. Goodman and W. Seth Carus, *The Future Battlefield and the Arab-Israeli Conflict* (New Brunswick, Transaction Publishers, 1990), Chapter 2.
9. A. George, 'Cut-price cruise missiles?' *The Middle East*, March 1993, pp. 15-16; J. Bermudez Jr., 'Ballistic Missiles in the Third World—Iran's Medium Range Missiles,' *JIR*, April 1992, pp. 147-152.
10. S. Chubin, 'Does Iran Want Nuclear Weapons?' *Survival*, Vol. 37, No. 1 (Spring 1995), pp. 86-104; CIA Nonproliferation Center, *The Weapons Proliferation Threat*, March 1995, p. 12.
11. On this threat, see: M.C. Libicki, 'DBK and its Consequences,' in S.E. Johnson and M.C. Libicki, eds, *Dominant Battlespace Knowledge: The Winning Edge* (Washington DC, National Defense University, 1995), pp. 27-58; 'What is Information Warfare?' *Strategic Forum* (National Defense University), No. 28 (May 1995).
12. In this context, it is worth noting that Iran has led the GCC states in use of the Internet. J. Cooper, 'The Middle East gets caught in the Internet,' *MEED*, 8 December 1995, pp. 2-3.

CHARTS

Chart 1
Military Capabilities
Iran-Iraq MBT Balance

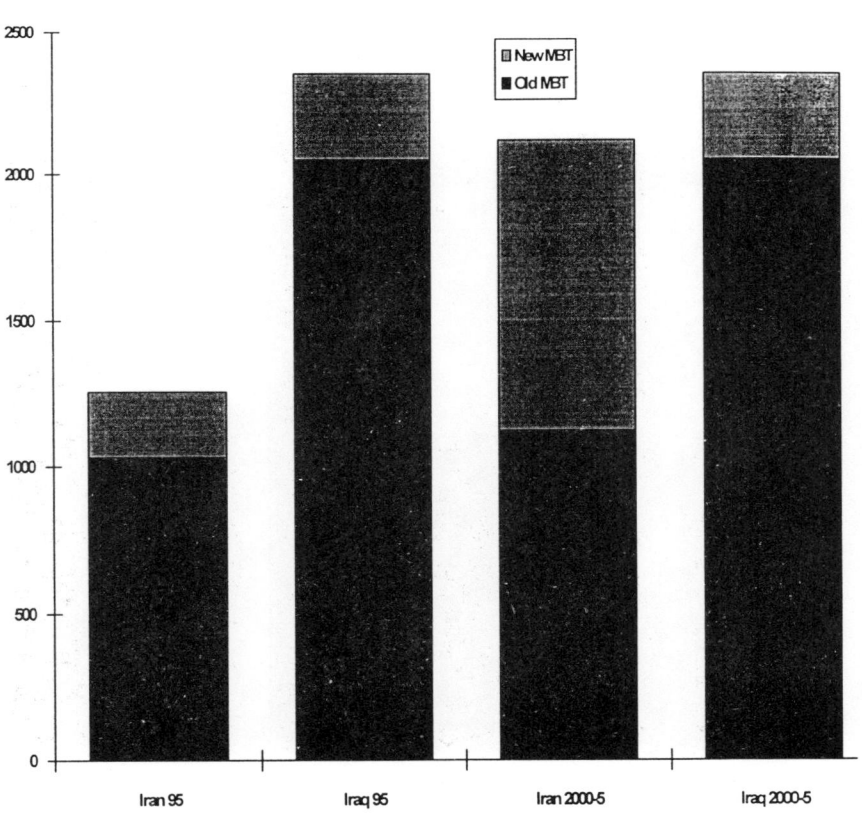

Note: Advanced MBT are T-72, T-80, M-84, M-60A3, Abrams M1A1/2, Leclerc, Challenger

The Changing Military Balance in the Gulf

Chart 2
Military Capabilities
Saudi-Iraq MBT Balance

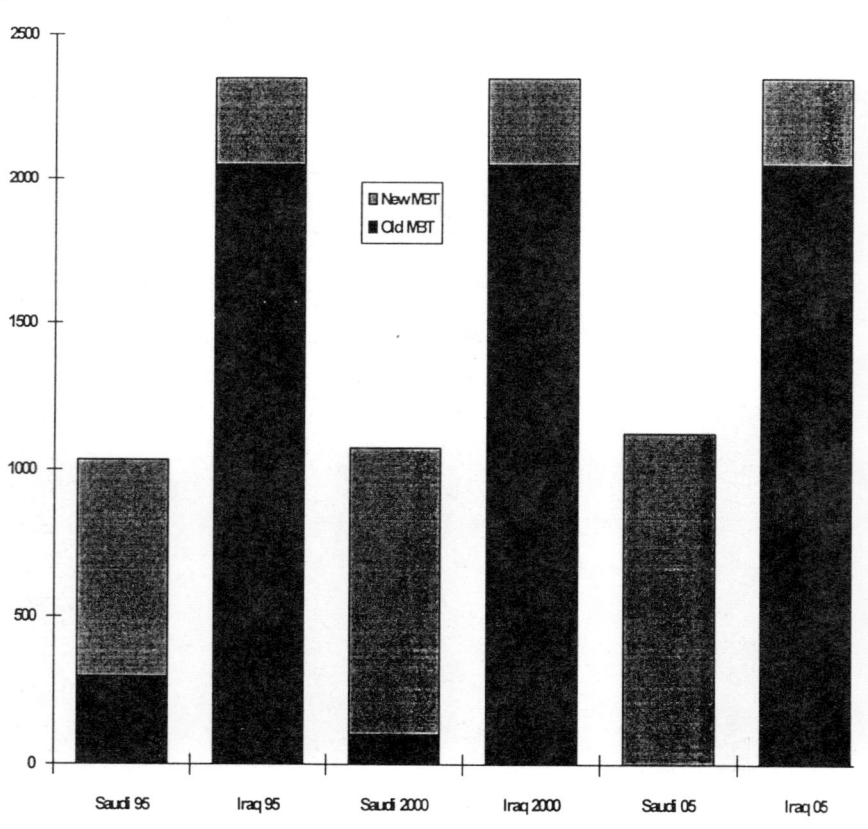

Note: Advanced MBT are T-72, T-80, M-84, M-60A3, Abrams M1A1/2, Leclerc, Challenger

Chart 3
**Military Capabilities
GCC-Iraq MBT Balance**

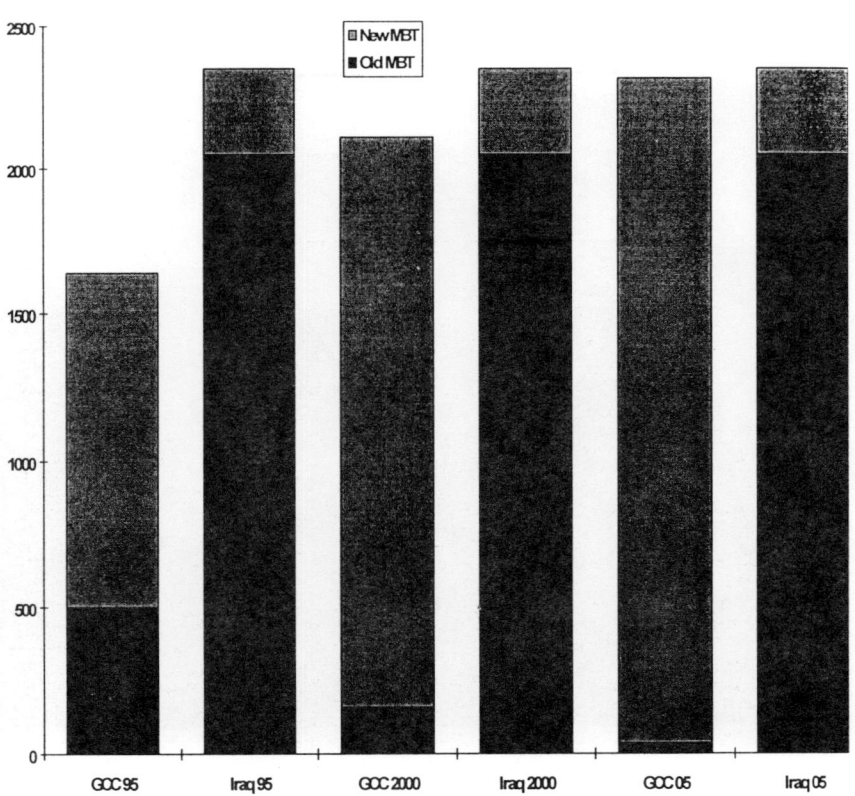

Note: Advanced MBT are T-72, T-80, M-84, M-60A3, Abrams M1A1/2, Leclerc, Challenger

Chart 4
**Military Capabilities
Iran-Iraq Aircraft Balance**

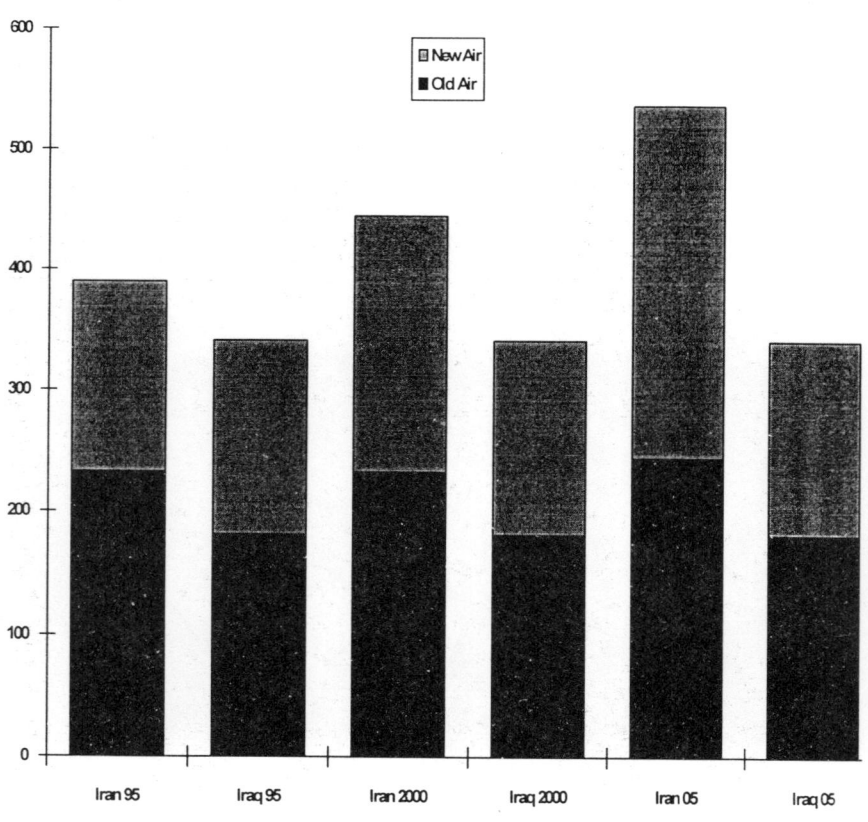

Note: Advanced aircraft are F-14, F-16, F-15, F-18, Tornado, Mirage F-1, Mirage 2000. Mirage 2000-5, MiG-29, MiG-23/27, MiG-31, Su-24, Tu-22

Charts

Chart 5
**Military Capabilities
Saudi-Iraq Aircraft Balance**

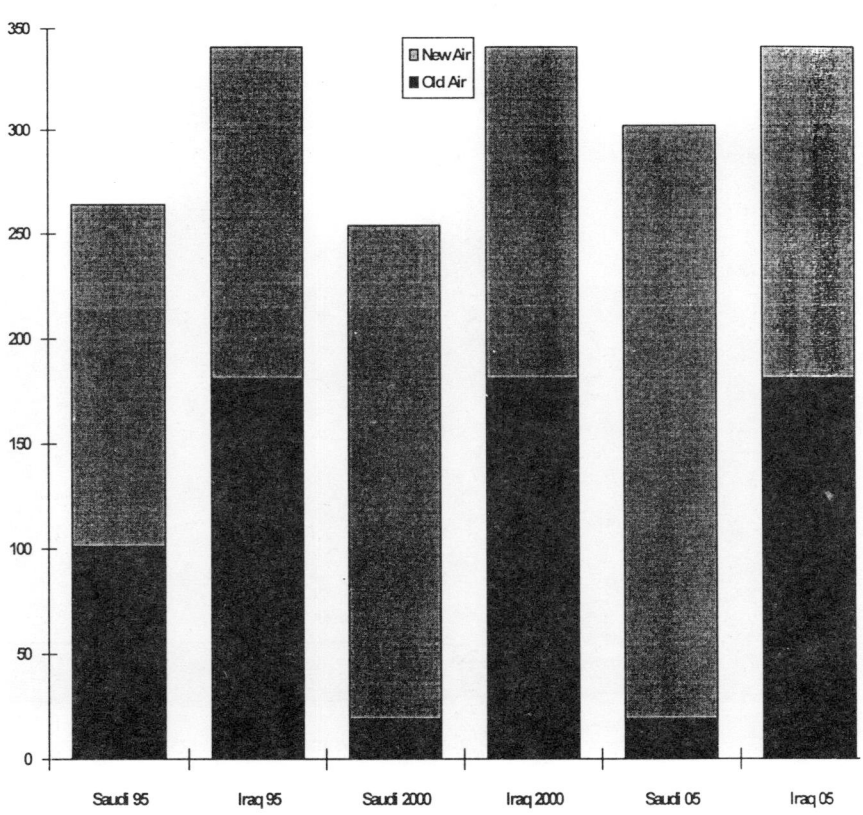

Note: Advanced aircraft are F-14, F-16, F-15, F-18, Tornado, Mirage F-1, Mirage 2000, Mirage 2000-5, MiG-29, MiG-25, MiG-23/27, MiG-31, Su-24, Tu-22

The Changing Military Balance in the Gulf

Chart 6
Military Capabilities
GCC-Iraq Aircraft Balance

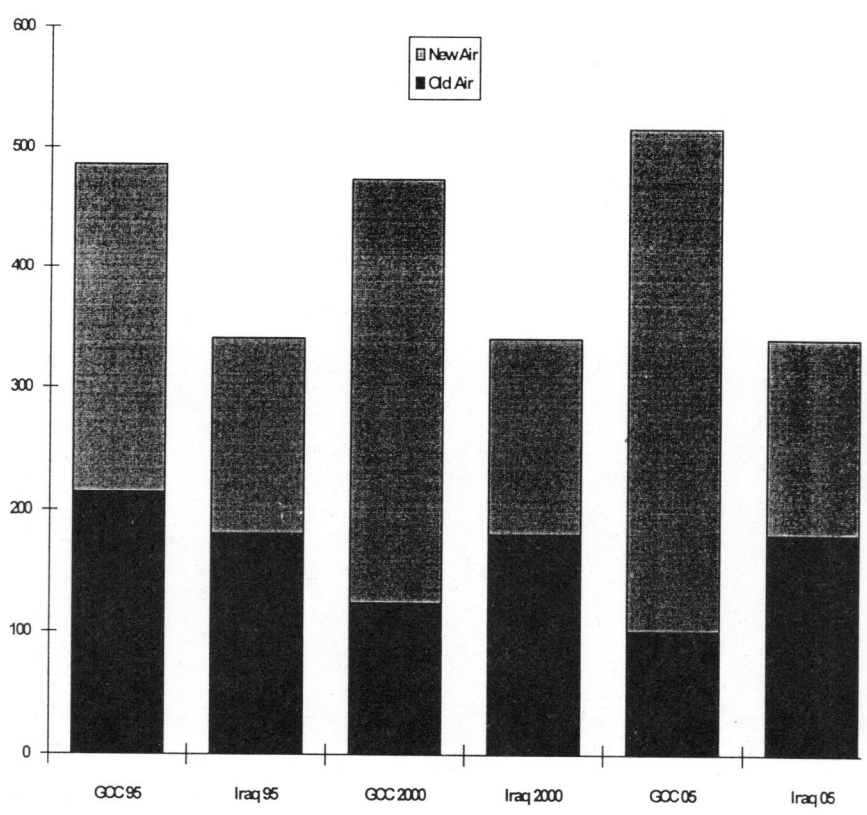

Note: Advanced aircraft are F-14, F-16, F-15, F-18, Tornado, Mirage F-1, Mirage 2000, Mirage 2000-5, MiG-29, MiG-25, MiG-23/27, MiG-31, Su-24, Tu-22

Chart 7
**Force Ratio in ADEs
Iran:Iraq**

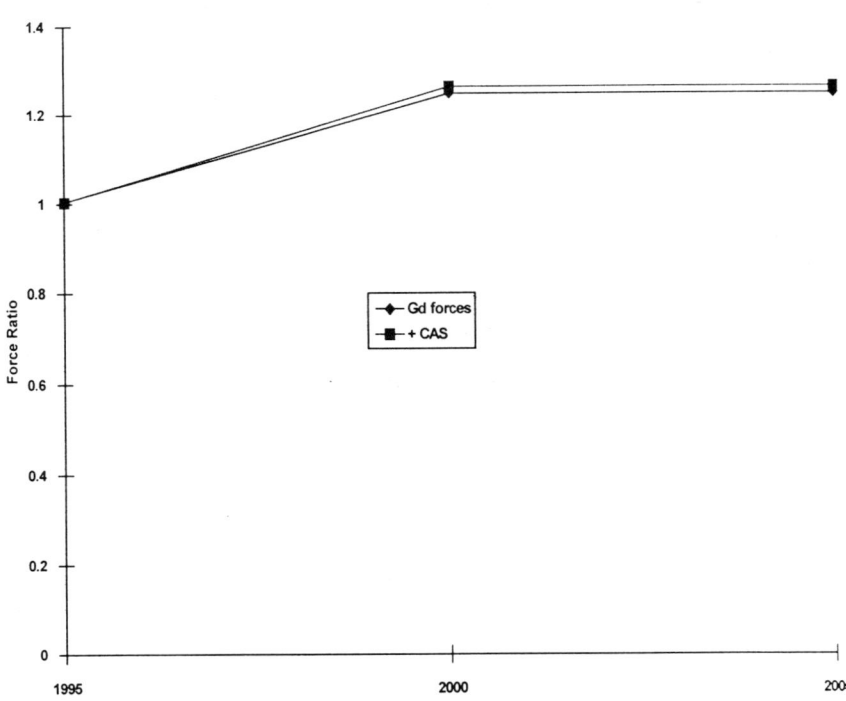

Chart 8
Force Ratio in ADEs
Iraq:Saudi Arabia

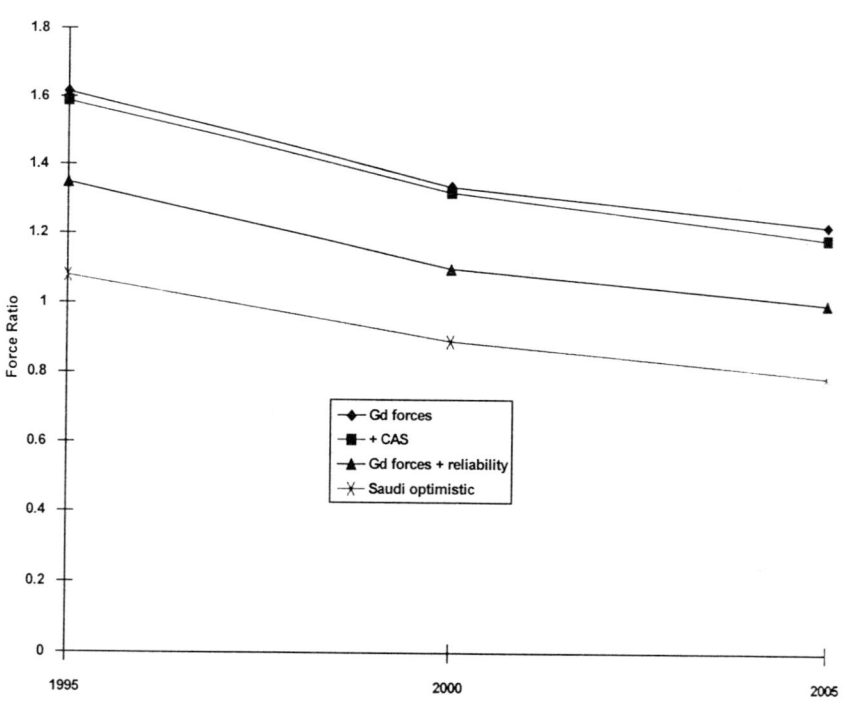

Chart 9
Force Ratio in ADEs
GCC:Iraq

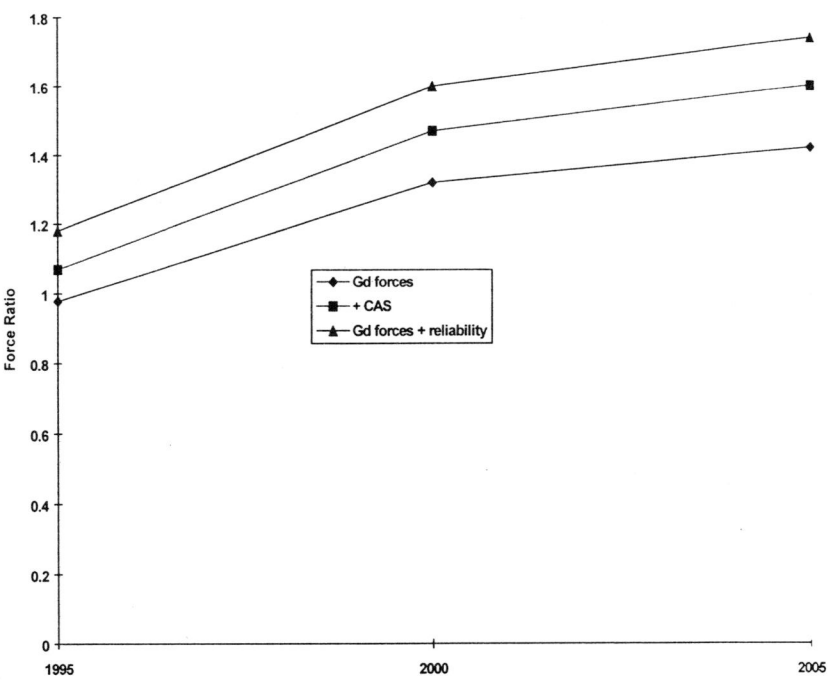

ize: small
APPENDICES

APPENDIX 1: GEO-STRATEGIC WEIGHTS

Figures are derived from successive editions of *The Military Balance* (IISS). The IISS's calculations of population, exchange rates and budgets are used for the sake of consistency.

Population
(million)

	Iran	Iraq	Saudi Arabia	Bahrain	Kuwait	Qatar	UAE	Oman
1975	33.81	11.49	5.5[1]	n/a	1.04	n/a	n/a	0.79
1985	45.2	15.4	11.6	0.42	1.71	0.30	1.3	1.3
1990	53.77	19.85	10.6	0.499	2.1	0.44	1.71	1.54
1995	64.8	21.04	18.61	0.57	1.51	0.54	1.83	1.88

GDP
(US$bn)

	Iran	Iraq	Saudi Arabia	Bahrain	Kuwait	Qatar	UAE	Oman
1975	56.8	13.4	24.8	n/a	11.0	n/a	n/a	n/a
1985	163.5	22.5	93.65	4.47	21.47	3.05	25.74	9.84
1990	59.49	40.78	87.97	4.01	25.3	7.05	33.67	9.16
1995	59.8	18.5	128.1	4.6	25.43	7.85	36.72	11.96

1. IISS puts figure at 5-6 million.

APPENDIX II: RELATIVE MILITARISATION

Figures are derived from successive editions of *The Military Balance* (IISS). The IISS's calculations of population, exchange rates and budgets are used for the sake of consistency.

Defence Expenditures (US$bn)

	Iran	Iraq	Saudi Arabia	Bahrain[1]	Kuwait	Qatar	UAE	Oman[2]
1975	9.5	1.191	6.77	n/a	0.230	n/a	n/a	0.768
1985	14.1	12.87	17.69	0.134[3]	1.64[4]	n/a[5]	2.04	2.1
1990	3.18	8.61	13.86[6]	0.193	1.5[7]	0.93	1.598	1.39
1995	2.46	2.7	13.2	0.253	2.91	0.33	1.88	1.9

Per Capita Defence Spending (US$)

	Iran	Iraq	Saudi Arabia	Bahrain	Kuwait	Qatar	UAE	Oman
1975	281	104	1231	n/a	221	n/a	n/a	972
1985	312	836	1525	319	959	n/a	1,569	1615
1990	59	434	1308	387	714	2114	930	902
1995	38	128	709	444	1927	611	1027	1010

Defence Spending as a Percentage of GDP (%)

	Iran	Iraq	Saudi Arabia	Bahrain	Kuwait	Qatar	UAE	Oman
1975	16.7	8.9	27.3	n/a	2.1	n/a	n/a	n/a
1985	8.6	57.2	18.9	3.0	7.6	n/a	7.9	21.3
1990	5.4	21.1	15.76	4.8	5.9	13.2	4.7	15.2
1995	4.1	14.6	10.3	5.5	11.4	4.2	5.1	15.9

Force Ratio (standing military personnel/1000)

	Iran	Iraq	Saudi Arabia	Bahrain	Kuwait	Qatar	UAE	Oman
1975	8.9	13.8	13	n/a	9.3	n/a	n/a	17.9
1985	23.3	54.9	5.8	6.7	7.0	20.0	33.1	16.5
1990	9.8	19.3	10.5	15.0	3.9	17.1	25.7	19.7
1995	9.8	18.2	8.7	18.8	11.0	20.6	38.3	23.1

Appendices

Notes

1. Excludes equipment costs and share of $1.8 bn GCC defence subsidy to Bahrain and Oman from 1984-1994.
2. Excludes share of $1.8 bn GCC defence subsidy to Bahrain and Oman from 1984-1994.
3. For 1986.
4. Excluding capital budget.
5. The figure given by IISS is $165.9bn. This is clearly a miscalculation so has been omitted.
6. Budget. Actual expenditure was $31.86bn, including contributions to allied war effort.
7. Budget. Actual expenditure was $13.1bn, including contributions to allied war effort.
8. Budget. Actual expenditure was $2.59bn, including contributions to allied war effort.

APPENDIX III: MILITARY CAPABILITY

Historical figures are based on successive editions of IISS, *The Military Balance*. Current and projected figures are based on calculations detailed in individual country sections. Projected figures are given in *italics*.

For all countries, where a range of figures has been given for total holdings in the relevant country section, the figure used here is a mid-point between high and low estimates. Projected figures for Iraq assume no significant arms imports before 2005.

Total Armed Forces
(000) Standing +(reserves)

	Iran[1]	Iraq	Saudi Arabia[2]	Bahrain	Kuwait	Qatar	UAE[3]	Oman	GCC Total
1975	300 (300)	158 (250)	71.5	n/a	9.7	n/a	n/a	14.15	n/a
1985	1054.5 (350)	845	67.5 (15)	2.8	12.0	6	43	21.5 (1)	152.8 (16)
1990	528 (350)	382.5 (650)	111.5 (20)	7.5	8.2	7.5	44	30.4	209.1 (20)
1995	633 (350)	382.5 (650)	162.5 (20)	10.7	16.6 (23.7)	11.1	70	43.5	314.4 (43.7)

Main Battle Tanks

	Iran	Iraq	Saudi Arabia[4]	Bahrain	Kuwait	Qatar	UAE	Oman	GCC Total
1975	1360	1290	325	n/a	100	n/a	n/a	-	n/a
1985	1000	4500	450	-	240	24	136	39	889
1990	700	2300	700	81	36	24	131	82	1054
1995	1255	2350	1035	113	245	24	133	87	1637
2000	2120	2350	1075	173	393	50	322	131	2144
2005	2120	2350	1125	173	393	50	462	113	2316

Advanced Main Battle Tanks
(T-72, T-80, M-84, M-60A3, Abrams M1A1/2, Leclerc, Challenger)[5]

	Iran	Iraq	Saudi Arabia[6]	Bahrain	Kuwait	Qatar	UAE	Oman	GCC Total
1995	225	300	740	113	225	-	2	57	1137
2000	1000	300	975	173	393	50	250	113	1954
2005	1000	300	1125	173	393	50	426	113	2280

Other Armoured Fighting Vehicles (AIFV/APC/ARV)

	Iran	Iraq	Saudi Arabia[7]	Bahrain	Kuwait	Qatar	UAE	Oman	GCC Total
1975	2000	1600	200	n/a	220	n/a	n/a	58	n/a
1985	1360	4000	1550	128	375	199	516	27	2795
1990	880	2900+	3740	142	70+	198	540	8	4698
1995	965	4400	4005	293	331	244	918	121	5912
2000	1592	4400	4665	318	850	248	918	181	7180
2005	1592	4400	4979	291	850	248	918	208	7494

Artillery (Towed & SP, excluding mortars)[8]

	Iran	Iraq	Saudi Arabia[9]	Bahrain	Kuwait	Qatar	UAE	Oman	GCC Total
1975	650	790	some	n/a	30	n/a	n/a	some	n/a
1985	600	5270	531+	8	38	14	88	93	772
1990	1000	1000+	533	22	11	14	97	75	752
1995	2884	1730	390	49	38	40	191	81	789
2000	2986	1730	390	49	56	40	191	66	792
2005	2986	1730	390	49	56	40	191	66	792

Multiple Rocket Launchers

	Iran	Iraq	Saudi Arabia	Bahrain	Kuwait	Qatar	UAE	Oman	GCC Total
1975	64	-	-	n/a	-	n/a	n/a	-	n/a
1985	65+	200	-	-	-	-	-	-	-
1990	105+	250	60	-	-	-	58	-	118
1995	425	250	60	9	-	4	48	-	121
2000	450	250	70	9	27	4	48	-	158
2005	450	250	99	9	27	4	48	-	187

SSM launchers

	Iran	Iraq	Saudi Arabia	Bahrain	Kuwait	Qatar	UAE	Oman	GCC Total
1975	-	some	-	n/a	-	n/a	n/a	-	n/a
1985	some	50	-	-	4	-	-	-	4
1990	some	26	10	-	-	-	-	-	10
1995	35	16	10	-	-	-	6	-	16
2000	35	-	10	-	-	-	6	-	16
2005	35	-	10	-	-	-	6	-	16

Armed Helicopters

	Iran	Iraq	Saudi Arabia	Bahrain	Kuwait	Qatar	UAE	Oman	GCC Total
1975	60	n/a	-	n/a	-	n/a	n/a	n/a	n/a
1985	12+	150?	-	-	23	2	7	n/a	n/a
1990	109	120	20	12	12	20	19	-	83
1995	105	123	27	9	16	20	30	-	102
2000	105	123	27	39	32	12	30	-	140
2005	105	123	51	42	40	12	30	-	175

Combat Aircraft

	Iran	Iraq	Saudi Arabia	Bahrain	Kuwait	Qatar	UAE	Oman	GCC Total
1975	317	299	97	n/a	33	n/a	n/a	44	n/a
1985	70	500	216	6	80	23	35	52	412
1990	213	261	253	24	34	18	100	57	486
1995	390	341	264	24	72	12	72	42	486
2000	444	341	254	24	64	18	72	42	474
2005	536	341	302	30	52	18	83	31	516

Advanced Combat Aircraft

(F-14, F-16, F-15, F-18, Tornado, Mirage F-1, Mirage 2000, Mirage 2000-5, MiG-29, MiG-25, MiG-23/27, MiG-31, Su-24, Tu-22)[10]

	Iran	Iraq	Saudi Arabia	Bahrain	Kuwait	Qatar	UAE	Oman	GCC Total
1995	158	160	163	12	52	6	39	-	272
2000	212	160	235	12	52	12	39	-	350
2005	292	160	283	30	40	12	50	-	415

Notes

1. Includes IRGC from 1985 figures on.
2. Includes SANG.
3. Includes Dubai forces.
4. Includes SANG.
5. In fact, the M1, Leclerc and Challenger are a generation more advanced than the other MBTs. This table therefore underestimates the superiority of armies with new generation tanks (i.e. the GCC states).
6. Includes SANG.
7. Includes SANG.
8. Includes SSR.
9. Includes SANG.
10. For the sake of simplicity, this table groups together aircraft which are in fact of different generations. The Mirage 2000-5, for instance, is far more effective than the Mirage F-1.

APPENDIX IV: ADE CALCULATIONS

WEI and category weights are taken from Mako, with input from Masaki. ADE score of 48 586 WUV from Masaki.[1] Values are estimated where necessary.

1995 Balance—Iran

No & Type of weapon	WEI	Cat. Wt. (offensive)	WUV
54 500 small arms[2]	1.00	1.00	54 500
20 *Zulfiqar*	1.14[3]	100	2280
225 T-72	1.14[4]	100	25 650
730 T-54/55, Type 59/69	0.89	100	64 970
100 T-62	1.03	100	10 300
145 Chieftain	1.14	100	16 530
120 M-47/8	0.87	100	10 440
105 M-60A1	1.0	100	10 500
90 PT-76	0.75	36	2430
55 Scorpion	0.88	36	1742
62 EE-9 Cascavel	0.75[5]	36	1674
30 BRDM-2	0.89	13	347
195 BMP-1	0.89	27	4686
100 BMP-2	1.00[6]	65	6500
543 APC	1.00	13	7059
1453 towed arty	0.44	64	40 917
231 SP arty	0.44	108	10 977
2875 Mortars	1.01	37	107 439
425 MRLs	0.54	108	24 786
1200 SSR	0.50[7]	100	60 000
600 RCL	0.21	27	3402
1570 ATGW	0.50	27	21 195
TOTAL WUV			**488 324**
TOTAL ADE			*ADE 10.051*

Iraq

No & Type of weapon	WEI	Cat. Wt. (offensive)	WUV
35,000 small arms[8]	1.00	1.00	35 000
400 T-62/72	1.11[9]	100	44 400
500 T-54/55, M-77, Type-59/69	0.89	100	44 500
1,450 assorted MBT	0.87	100	126 150
1,500 ARV	0.75	36	40 500
900 BMP-1/2	0.93[10]	40[11]	33 480
2,000 APC	1.00	13	26 000
1,500 towed arty	0.44	64	42 240
230 SP arty	0.44	108	10 930
1,500 Mortars	1.01	37	56 055
250 MRLs	0.54	108	14 580
? RCL (assume 1,000)	0.21	27	**5670**
? ATGW (assume 500)	0.50	27	**6750**
TOTAL WUV *TOTAL ADE*			486 255 *ADE 10.008*

Saudi Arabia

No & Type of weapon	WEI	Cat. Wt. (offensive)	WUV
13 000 small arms[12]	1.00	1.00	13 000
315 Abrams M1	1.25[13]	100	39 375
425 M60A3	1.15[14]	100	48 875
295 AMX-30	0.93	55	15 089
390 ARV	0.85[15]	36	11 934
400 M2 Bradley	1.25	65	32 500
1865 AIFV	1.00	40	74 600
1350 M113	1.00	13	17 550
160 towed arty	0.44	64	4506
230 SP arty	0.44	108	10 930
288 Mortars	1.01	37	10 763
60 MRLs	0.54	108	3499
425 RCL	0.21	27	2410
1170 ATGW	0.50	27	15 795
TOTAL WUV *TOTAL ADE*			**300 826** *ADE 6.192*

Other GCC

No & Type of weapon	WEI	Cat. Wt. (offensive)	WUV
11,700 small arms[16]	1.00	1.00	11 700
50 Abrams M1	1.25[17]	100	6250
2 Leclerc	1.25[18]	100	250
12 Challenger	1.25[19]	100	1500
158 M60A3	1.15[20]	100	18 170
6 M60A1	1.00	100	600
211 M-84/T-72/OF-40	1.14[21]	100	24 054
24 Chieftain	1.14	100	2736
119 AMX-30	0.93	55	6087
299 ARV	0.85[22]	36	9149
8 Warrior	1.25[23]	65	650
406 BMP-3	1.25[24]	65	32 988
46 BMP-2	1.00[25]	65	2990
76 AIFV	1.00	40	3040
1,056 APC	1.00	13	13 728
220 towed arty	0.44	64	6195
179 SP arty	0.44	108	8506
319 Mortars	1.01	37	11 921
52 MRLs	0.54	108	3033
516 RCL	0.21	27	2926
593 ATGW	0.50	27	8006
TOTAL WUV *TOTAL ADE*			**174 479** *ADE 3.591*

2000 Balance

Iran

No & Type of weapon	WEI	Cat.Wt. (offensive)	WUV
54 500 small arms[26]	1.00	1.00	54 500
20 *Zulfiqar*	1.14[27]	100	2280
1000 T-72	1.14[28]	100	114 000
730 T-54/55, Type 59/69	0.89	100	64 970
100 T-62	1.03	100	10 300
145 Chieftain	1.14	100	16 530
120 M-47/8	0.87	100	10 440
105 M-60A1	1.0	100	10 500
90 PT-76	0.75	36	2430
55 Scorpion	0.88	36	1742
62 EE-9 Cascavel	0.75[29]	36	1674
30 BRDM-2	0.89	13	347
195 BMP-1	0.89	27	4686
500 BMP-2	1.00[30]	65	32 500
543 APC	1.00	13	7059
1555 towed arty	0.44	64	43 789
231 SP arty	0.44	108	10 977
2875 Mortars	1.01	37	107 439
450 MRLs	0.54	108	26 244
1200 SSR	0.50[31]	100	60 000
600 RCL[32]	0.21	27	3402
1570 ATGW[33]	0.50	27	21 195
TOTAL WUV *TOTAL ADE*		. .	**607 004** *ADE 12.493*

Iraq[34]

No & Type of weapon	WEI	Cat. Wt. (offensive)	WUV
35 000 small arms[35]	1.00	1.00	35 000
400 T-62/72	1.11[36]	100	44 400
500 T-54/55, M-77, Type-59/69	0.89	100	44 500
1450 assorted MBT	0.87	100	126 150
1500 ARV	0.75	36	40 500
900 BMP-1/2	0.93[37]	40[38]	33 480
2000 APC	1.00	13	26 000
1500 towed arty	0.44	64	42 240
230 SP arty	0.44	108	10 930
1500 Mortars	1.01	37	56 055
250 MRLs	0.54	108	14 580
? RCL (assume 1,000)	0.21	27	**5670**
? ATGW (assume 500)	0.50	27	**6750**
TOTAL WUV *TOTAL ADE*			**486 255** *ADE 10.008*

The Changing Military Balance in the Gulf

Saudi Arabia

No & Type of weapon	WEI	Cat. Wt. (offensive)	WUV
16 500 small arms[39]	1.00	1.00	16 500
550 Abrams M1	1.25[40]	100	68 750
425 M60A3	1.15[41]	100	48 875
145 AMX-30	0.93	55	7417
390 ARV	0.85[42]	36	11 934
550 M2 Bradley	1.25	65	44 688
2375 AIFV	1.00	40	95 000
1350 M113	1.00	13	17550
160 towed arty	0.44	64	4506
230 SP arty	0.44	108	10 930
411 Mortars	1.01	37	15 359
70 MRLs	0.54	108	4082
425 RCL	0.21	27	2410
1170 ATGW	0.50	27	15 795
TOTAL WUV **TOTAL ADE**			**363 796** *ADE 7.488*

Other GCC

No & Type of weapon	WEI	Cat. Wt. (offensive)	WUV
11 200 small arms[43]	1.00	1.00	11 200
218 Abrams M1	1.25[44]	100	27 250
300 Leclerc[45]	1.25[46]	100	37 500
18 Challenger	1.25[47]	100	2250
268 M60A3	1.15[48]	100	30 820
6 M60A1	1.00	100	600
211 M-84/T-72/OF-40	1.14[49]	100	24 054
12 Chieftain	1.14	100	1368
36 AMX-30	0.93	55	1841
389 ARV	0.85[50]	36	11 903
254 Warrior	1.25[51]	65	20 638
466 BMP-3	1.25[52]	65	37 863
46 BMP-2	1.00[53]	65	2990
162 AIFV	1.00	40	6480
1191 APC	1.00	13	15 483
186 towed arty	0.44	64	5238
215 SP arty	0.44	108	10 217
319 Mortars	1.01	37	11 921
88 MRLs	0.54	108	5132
516 RCL	0.21	27	2926
593 ATGW	0.50	27	8006
TOTAL WUV			**275 680**
TOTAL ADE			*ADE 5.674*

The Changing Military Balance in the Gulf

2005 Balance

Iran

No & Type of weapon	WEI	Cat. Wt. (offensive)	WUV
54 500 small arms[54]	1.00	1.00	54 500
20 *Zulfiqar*	1.14[55]	100	2280
1000 T-72	1.14[56]	100	114 000
730 T-54/55, Type 59/69	0.89	100	64 970
100 T-62	1.03	100	10 300
145 Chieftain	1.14	100	16 530
120 M-47/8	0.87	100	10 440
105 M-60A1	1.0	100	10 500
90 PT-76	0.75	36	2430
55 Scorpion	0.88	36	1742
62 EE-9 Cascavel	0.75[57]	36	1674
30 BRDM-2	0.89	13	347
195 BMP-1	0.89	27	4686
500 BMP-2	1.00[58]	65	32 500
543 APC	1.00	13	7059
1555 towed arty	0.44	64	43 789
231 SP arty	0.44	108	10 977
2875 Mortars	1.01	37	107 439
450 MRLs	0.54	108	26 244
1200 SSR	0.50[59]	100	60 000
600 RCL[60]	0.21	27	3402
1570 ATGW[61]	0.50	27	21 195
TOTAL WUV **TOTAL ADE**			**607 004** *ADE* *12.493*

Iraq[62]

No & Type of weapon	WEI	Cat. Wt. (offensive)	WUV
35 000 small arms[63]	1.00	1.00	35 000
400 T-62/72	1.11[64]	100	44 400
500 T-54/55, M-77, Type-59/69	0.89	100	44 500
1450 assorted MBT	0.87	100	126 150
1500 ARV	0.75	36	40 500
900 BMP-1/2	0.93[65]	40[66]	33 480
2000 APC	1.00	13	26 000
1500 towed arty	0.44	64	42 240
230 SP arty	0.44	108	10930
1500 Mortars	1.01	37	56 055
250 MRLs	0.54	108	14 580
? RCL (assume 1000)	0.21	27	**5670**
? ATGW (assume 500)	0.50	27	**6750**
TOTAL WUV *TOTAL ADE*			**486 255** *ADE* *10.008*

Saudi Arabia

No & Type of weapon	WEI	Cat. Wt. (offensive)	WUV
20 000 small arms[67]	1.00	1.00	20 000
700 Abrams M1	1.25[68]	100	87 500
425 M60A3	1.15[69]	100	48 875
390 ARV	0.85[70]	36	11 934
700 M2 Bradley	1.25	65	56 875
2539 AIFV	1.00	40	101 560
1350 M113	1.00	13	17 550
160 towed arty	0.44	64	4506
230 SP arty	0.44	108	10 930
363 Mortars	1.01	37	13 565
99 MRLs	0.54	108	5774
425 RCL	0.21	27	2410
1170 ATGW	0.50	27	15 795
TOTAL WUV **TOTAL ADE**			**397 274** *ADE 8.177*

Other GCC

No & Type of weapon	WEI	Cat. Wt. (offensive)	WUV
10 700 small arms[71]	1.00	1.00	10 700
218 Abrams M1	1.25[72]	100	27 250
440 Leclerc[73]	1.25[74]	100	55 000
18 Challenger	1.25[75]	100	2250
268 M60A3	1.15[76]	100	30 820
247 M-84/T-72/T-80/OF-40	1.14[77]	100	28 158
362 ARV	0.85[78]	36	11 077
254 Warrior	1.25[79]	65	20 638
466 BMP-3	1.25[80]	65	37 863
46 BMP-2	1.00[81]	65	2990
162 AIFV	1.00	40	6480
1,172 APC	1.00	13	15 236
186 towed arty	0.44	64	5238
215 SP arty	0.44	108	10 217
319 Mortars	1.01	37	11 921
88 MRLs	0.54	108	5132
516 RCL	0.21	27	2926
593 ATGW	0.50	27	8006
TOTAL WUV *TOTAL ADE*			**291 902** *ADE 6.008*

Notes

1. Mako, *US Ground Forces and the Defense of Central Europe*; Masaki, 'The Korean Question: Assessing the Military Balance,' *Security Studies*.
2. Based on one tenth of active army manpower as cited in IISS, *The Military Balance*. Also includes 20,000 from IRGC, assuming one fifth are in front line infantry.

3. Estimated same as T-72.
4. Estimated same as Chieftain.
5. Estimated.
6. Estimated same as KIFV in Masaki.
7. Estimated.
8. Based on one tenth of active army manpower as cited in IISS, *The Military Balance*.
9. Weighted average, assumes 300 T-72 and 100 T-62.
10. Weighted average, assumes 2/3rd BMP1.
11. Weighted average, assumes 2/3rd BMP1.
12. Based on one tenth of active army manpower as cited in IISS, *The Military Balance* and one-fifth of SANG combat personnel (6,000).
13. Estimated.
14. Estimated.
15. Estimated.
16. Based on one tenth of active army manpower as cited in IISS, *The Military Balance*. Bahrain: 850, Kuwait: 1,000, Qatar: 850, UAE: 6,500, Oman: 2,500.
17. Estimated.
18. Estimated.
19. Estimated.
20. Estimated.
21. Estimated same as Chieftain.
22. Estimated.
23. Estimated.
24. Estimated.
25. Estimated same as KIFV in Masaki
26. Based on one tenth of active army manpower as cited in IISS, *The Military Balance*. Also includes 20,000 from IRGC, assuming one fifth are in front line infantry.
27. Estimated.
28. Estimated.
29. Estimated.
30. Estimated same as KIFV in Masaki.
31. Estimated.
32. Jane's figures.
33. Jane's figures.
34. Assumes no deterioration of equipment over time although this would be likely given the lack of spares and the need to cannibalise hardware.

Appendices

35. Based on one tenth of active army manpower as cited in IISS, *The Military Balance*.
36. Weighted average, assumes 300 T-72 and 100 T-62.
37. Weighted average, assumes 2/3rd BMP1.
38. Weighted average, assumes 2/3rd BMP1.
39. Assumes Saudi army expands total manpower to 85,000 and that SANG expands total active combat manpower to 40,000. Based on one tenth of active army manpower and one-fifth of SANG combat personnel (8,000).
40. Estimated.
41. Estimated.
42. Estimated.
43. Based on one tenth of active army manpower. Assumes Kuwait adds 5,000 soldiers and UAE cuts 10,000. Bahrain: 850, Kuwait: 1,500, Qatar: 850, UAE: 5,500, Oman: 2,500.
44. Estimated.
45. Assumes Qatar purchases Leclercs.
46. Estimated.
47. Estimated.
48. Estimated.
49. Estimated same as Chieftain.
50. Estimated.
51. Estimated.
52. Estimated.
53. Estimated same as KIFV in Masaki
54. Based on one tenth of active army manpower as cited in IISS, *The Military Balance*. Also includes 20,000 from IRGC, assuming one fifth are in front line infantry.
55. Estimated.
56. Estimated.
57. Estimated.
58. Estimated same as KIFV in Masaki.
59. Estimated.
60. Jane's figures.
61. Jane's figures.
62. Assumes no deterioration of equipment over time.
63. Based on one tenth of active army manpower as cited in IISS, *The Military Balance*.
64. Weighted average, assumes 300 T-72 and 100 T-62.
65. Weighted average, assumes 2/3rd BMP1.
66. Weighted average, assumes 2/3rd BMP1.

67. Assumes Saudi army expands total manpower to 100,000 and that SANG expands total active combat manpower to 50,000. Based on one tenth of active army manpower and one-fifth of SANG combat personnel (10,000).
68. Estimated.
69. Estimated.
70. Estimated.
71. Based on one tenth of active army manpower. Assumes Kuwait adds a further 5000 soldiers and UAE cuts a further 10 000. Bahrain: 850, Kuwait: 2000, Qatar: 850, UAE: 4,500, Oman: 2,500.
72. Estimated.
73. Assumes Qatar purchases Leclercs.
74. Estimated.
75. Estimated.
76. Estimated.
77. Estimated same as Chieftain.
78. Estimated.
79. Estimated.
80. Estimated.
81. Estimated same as KIFV in Masaki

APPENDIX V: EFFECT OF CLOSE AIR SUPPORT

This model of the effect of Close Air Support (CAS) is taken from Posen.[1] It is based on a simple formula to calculate the numbers of ADEs destroyed by CAS over a period of time. In Posen's words 'the tacair formula is straightforward. For each sortie the total number of aircraft leaving base is multiplied by 0.95 (i.e.. five per cent attrition) and then by the kill rate to come up with a total kill per sortie. Those aircraft that have survived the sortie ... are run through the equation for the next sortie. Second sortie survivors are run through the third, etc.'[2]

In order to apply the model, this study assumes that, in an Iran-Iraq conflict, the Iranian and Iraqi air forces cancel each other out and their CAS is free to operate over the battlefield. In the case of a conflict between Iraq and Saudi Arabia and/or the GCC states it is assumed that the GCC air forces dominate the airspace and prevent half of Iraq's CAS from operating.

When applying his model to Europe, Posen assumed that higher NATO investments in training and advanced avionics and weapons systems would give NATO CAS a higher kill and sortie rate than Warsaw Pact CAS. This study assumes the same for GCC air forces. This is not to suggest either that the GCC air forces match NATO standards or that Iran or Iraq match Warsaw Pact standards. In reality, all would perform significantly less well than their developed nation counterparts. It is nonetheless appropriate to retain these figures since it is relative rather than absolute performance that is of interest.[3]

CAS Performance

	Saudi/GCC	Iran & Iraq
Attrition	5%	5%
Kills per sortie	0.5	0.35
Daily sortie rate	2	1

For the Iran-Iraq scenario the CAS equation is reiterated for a period of two weeks and the kills converted into ADEs, assuming one third of kills are of an average MBT, one third are an average AIFV and one third are an average APC.[4]

For the Iraq-Saudi scenario the same procedure is followed but only for one week since any major conflict is less likely to persist before foreign intervention affects the balance.

Tactical Air Strengths, 1995

	Iran	Iraq	Saudi	Other GCC
Fixed Wing	141[5]	118[6]	76[7]	72[8]
Helicopter	56[9]	83[10]	27	50[11]
Total	*197*	*201*	*103*	*122*

Tactical Air Strengths, 2000

	Iran	Iraq	Saudi	Other GCC
Fixed Wing	141	118	50[12]	72[13]
Helicopter	56	83	27	81[14]
Total	*197*	*201*	*77*	*153*

Tactical Air Strengths, 2005

	Iran	Iraq	Saudi	Other GCC
Fixed Wing	141	118	65[15]	76[16]
Helicopter	56	83	51	89[17]
Total	*197*	*201*	*116*	*165*

Appendices

Notes

1. Posen, *Inadvertent Escalation*, pp. 101-106 and Appendix 2.
2. Posen, *Inadvertent Escalation*, p. 104, note 67. The 5 per cent attrition is probably unrealistically high. On the eve of Desert Storm, US Air Force planners estimated an attrition rate of 3 per cent on the first day and 0.5 per cent on subsequent days. Gordon and Trainor, *The Generals' War*, p. 92.
3. In addition, this model is not flexible enough to capture the qualitative changes in CAS assets, notably the acquisition of AH-64 Apaches by some of the GCC states. Nonetheless, it will serve its purpose as a rough indicator of the impact of CAS.
4. This weighted average makes each AFV killed worth 47 WUV.
5. Assumes half of US aircraft are unserviceable. Serviceable aircraft counted are: 25 F-4s, 28 F-5s, 37 Su-22, 24 MiG-23, 20 F-7 and 7 Su-25s. Assumes that more sophisticated FGAs are reserved for interdiction and strike missions.
6. Assumes three quarters of aircraft are serviceable. Serviceable aircraft counted are: 15 F-7, 20 MiG-21, 20 MiG-23BN, 41 Su-20/22 and 22 Su-25.
7. Assumes 64 F-5 and 12 Tornado IDS used for CAS.
8. Assumes 8 F-5s from Bahrain, 12 Hawk and 8 Strikemaster from Kuwait, 6 Alpha Jet from Qatar, 18 Hawk 102 from UAE and 10 Hawk and 10 Strikemaster from Oman.
9. Assumes half of US aircraft (AH-1) are unserviceable.
10. Assumes two thirds are serviceable.
11. Assumes 6 AB-212 from Bahrain, 16 Gazelles from Kuwait, 8 Gazelles from Qatar, 10 Gazelles and 10 Apaches from the UAE.
12. Assumes F-5 phased out but 20 Hawk and 30 Tornado used for CAS.
13. Assumes 8 F-5s from Bahrain, 12 Hawk and 8 FA-18 from Kuwait, 6 Alpha Jet from Qatar, 18 Hawk 102 from UAE and 10 Hawk and 10 Strikemaster from Oman.
14. Assumes 6 AB-212 and 15 Cobras from Bahrain, 16 Gazelles and 16 Apaches from Kuwait, 8 Gazelles from Qatar, 10 Gazelles and 10 Apaches from the UAE.
15. Assumes 20 Hawk and 45 Tornado used for CAS.
16. Assumes 10 F-16s from Bahrain, 12 Hawk and 8 FA-18 from Kuwait, 6 Alpha Jet from Qatar, 18 Hawk 102 and 12 new strike aircraft from UAE and 10 Hawk from Oman.
17. Assumes 6 Apaches and 15 Cobras from Bahrain, 16 Gazelles and 24 Apaches from Kuwait, 8 Gazelles from Qatar, 10 Gazelles and 10 Apaches from the UAE.